Rockhounding
California

Gail A. Butler

Consulting Editor
W.R.C. Shedenhelm

FALCONGUIDES ®

GUILFORD, CONNECTICUT
HELENA, MONTANA
AN IMPRINT OF THE GLOBE PEQUOT PRESS

FALCONGUIDES®

Copyright © 1995 Morris Book Publishing, LLC
Previously published by Falcon Publishing, Inc.

Falcon, FalconGuides, and Outfit Your Mind, are registered trademarks of Morris
Book Publishing, LLC.

All photos by Gail Butler unless credited otherwise.
Front cover photo by: Rick Wicker

Cataloging-in-Publication Data on file at the Library of Congress.

ISBN 978-1-56044-639-2

Printed in the United States of America
First Edition/Tenth Printing

CONTENTS

Appendices

ACKNOWLEDGMENTS

There are many people who have made the writing of this book possible. To list all of them would require another whole volume. So I will start at the beginning and be as brief as possible.

I thank my grandfather, Alvin B. Butler, a prospector. When I was very young, he nurtured my interest in rockhounding by bringing me wonderful rock and mineral specimens he found on gold prospecting trips.

Thanks to James R. Mitchell for his rockhounding guide, **Gem Trails of California**, that lead me on my first trips into the wilderness to look for rocks years ago.

Thanks to the members of the Bear Gulch Rock Club of Ontario, California, who further encouraged my interest in both rockhounding and in turning my found stones into lovely, lapidary treasures. I am also grateful for their companionship and fun on many rockhounding trips. A special thanks also to member Bob Kawka who strongly encouraged me to write my first article.

I wish to thank W.R.C. Shedenhelm, editor emeritus of **ROCK & GEM MAGAZINE**, who published my first article in 1985 and then said, "Keep 'em coming." I also thank him for his on-going encouragement, humor, winefests, humor, sharing of books and maps, humor, and his valuable advice...and of course, his humor. It was greatly due to him that this guide has been written.

To my mother, Barbara Parry, a heartfelt thanks from me, my feline friends, and plants for feeding and watering them while I was gallivanting about the state taking photos and detailing site write-ups for this book. Thanks also for picking up the tons of mail that were delivered while I was away.

Thank you, thank you to my dear friends and partners, Mo and Ed Hemler, who tracked my gallivantings and were prepared to mount a rescue mission should I not return or check in at the appointed times.

Thank you to Scooter Patrick, mechanic extraordinaire, who kept my Suzuki running in top form. In a year of running about the state, often in the remotest reaches of wilderness by myself, the "Sooz" never failed.

Thank you to my aunt and uncle, Peggy and Ed Butler, who allowed me to use their home as the base from which all the northern sites were collected and for joining me on some of the expeditions. Thank you also to my father, Al Butler, and his betrothed, Sandy Olsen, for more bed and board during my travels.

Thank you to the San Diego Mineral and Gem Society and their junior members for inviting me to accompany them on a trip to one of the sites listed in this guide. I appreciate their ongoing mailings of the **Pegmatite Bulletin**, which contains valuable information regarding legislation that effects rockhounding, some of which has gone into this guide.

Thanks to the members of the Mount Jura Gem and Mineral Club who gave me directions and information for some of the northern sites used in this guide.

Thank you to Nancy and Howard Fisher, of Opal Hill Fire Agate Mine, for teaching me their techniques of mining for fire agate.

Thanks to Norm and Mike Grant for many lovely and golden hours spent prospecting for gold at their Rich Bar claim.

Thanks go to Herman Schob for his company on several of the southern site trips and for the information he sent on some of the northern sites.

Thank you to Jude' Kendrick, with whom I discovered and explored some of the desert sites that subsequently ended up in this book.

Thank you to Jim Nelson, president of the California Federation of Mineralogical Societies, and to Renata Williams-Bever, the executive secretary, for supplying the club listings for this guide and other information, and to Susan Haverland, current editor of **ROCK & GEM MAGAZINE**.

SITE LOCATIONS MAP

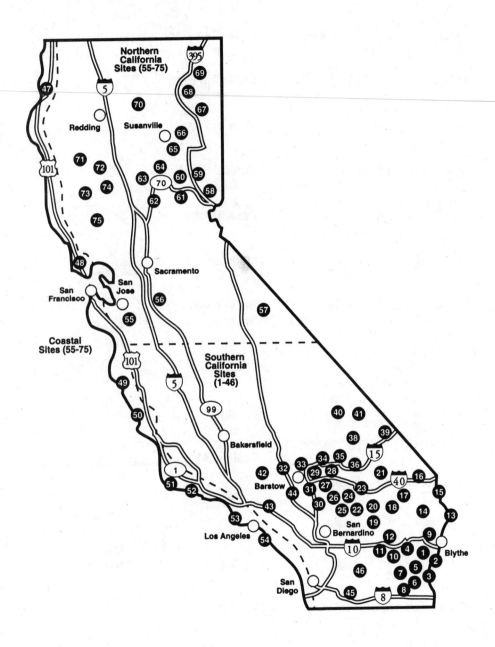

MAP LEGEND

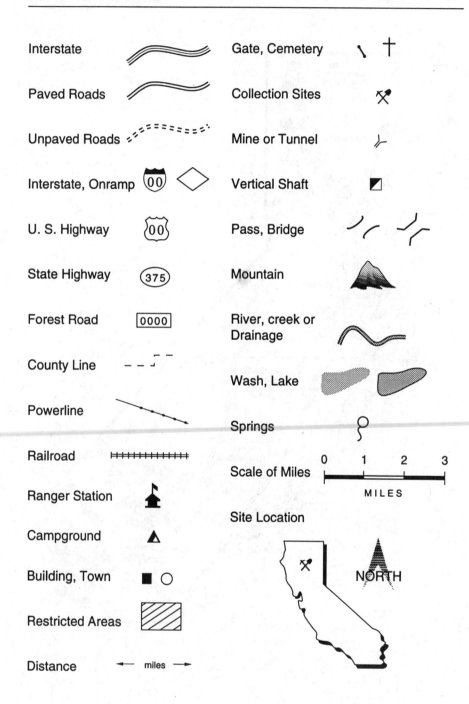

Interstate		Gate, Cemetery	
Paved Roads		Collection Sites	
Unpaved Roads		Mine or Tunnel	
Interstate, Onramp	00	Vertical Shaft	
U. S. Highway	00	Pass, Bridge	
State Highway	375	Mountain	
Forest Road	0000	River, creek or Drainage	
County Line		Wash, Lake	
Powerline		Springs	
Railroad		Scale of Miles	0 1 2 3 MILES
Ranger Station		Site Location	
Campground			
Building, Town		NORTH	
Restricted Areas			
Distance	miles		

PREFACE

About This Book

The object of this book is to provide rockhounds with as much up-to-date information as possible to enable them to go out into the field and collect the many interesting gem and mineral treasures that abound in California.

Many of the gem and mineral guides for California are years, sometimes decades, out of date. Legislation continually changes land status and access to areas in California. New roads have been built, altering directions and mileages to many collecting sites.

In most cases the author has visited the sites listed to check on mileages, status, and availability of collecting material. Several sites were contributed by friends of the author, who also enjoy a weekend of rockhounding and have their favorite collecting spots.

The information in this book is presented so that rockhounds and mineral collectors, whether new to the hobby or not, will be able to use this guide to find interesting gems and minerals for their collections and lapidary projects.

By no means does this book list all of the mineral or collecting sites in California. It does list those that the author has enjoyed visiting and which she has found to be accessible and enjoyable. These sites also contain a diversity of gem and mineral material. Some sites are included because they are old favorites among rockhounds and are traditional weekend camping and gathering spots. Some were discovered by the author.

Commercial mines are not listed in the site write-ups, as they are not generally accessible to rockhounds. A few that allow occasional collecting are listed under **Rockhound Access to Commercial Mines.**

Also listed are published sources that were used in the writing of this book or which the author feels may be of interest to those who would like more information or knowledge concerning rockhounding.

Lastly, this book is dedicated to all rockhounds past, present, and future and to the enjoyable hobby of rockhounding. May it continue!

California poppy—the state flower.

INTRODUCTION

California! Land of earthquakes and wind-driven wildfires, scorching deserts, wave-washed beaches, and breathtaking mountain vistas. If any one word could best describe the state of California, that word would be **variety**. California has something to offer everyone.

Several friendly arguments exist on how California received its name. One favorite is that the name is taken from the words "kali," meaning "high," and "forno," meaning "hills." Another argument states that the name comes from the latin "calida fornax," that translated means "hot furnace." Still another theory maintains that the Indian word "tchalifalni-al," roughly meaning "the sandy land against the water," is the true source of California's name. While all these arguments seem plausible enough, the last one appears most reasonable due to the fact that California has a mostly temperate climate and more than 1,200 miles of coastline.

The name "California" often evokes historic goldrush days and images of crusty, sourdough miners. Gold is, not surprisingly, the state mineral and is still avidly sought on weekends by recreational gold prospectors.

The California poppy, the golden-hued state flower, is best seen in early spring brightly adorning the hillsides. The endearing California valley quail, with its curious top knot and white facial markings, is the state bird. Benitoite, a rare, transparent blue crystal found only in California, is the state gemstone.

Although known mostly for its history of gold production, California also yields a wide variety of other valuable mineral commodities. Ghost towns and abandoned mines testify to a rich history of precious metals mining, not only of gold but copper and silver.

Modern day mines, some still producing gold, also extract other ores and minerals, such as iron, lead, tungsten, zinc, quick silver, talc, chromite, and borate minerals.

California is truly a mineralogical wonderland and a virtual haven for rock and gem collectors. Practically every known mineral exists in some quantity somewhere in California.

The Landscape

No single type of terrain can best describe the geographic and geologic diversity that is California. The total landmass of California is 158,297 square miles.

Moving from the central and southeastern edge of California, westward toward the mighty Pacific Ocean, we first encounter deserts at the southern end and up into the central portion of the state. These are the Mojave and Colorado deserts and the infamous Death Valley.

Transverse mountain ranges, named because they lie contrary to the prevailing northwesterly fabric of the state's landmass, create a barrier to coastal moisture, resulting in these thirsty but austerely beautiful and mineral-rich desert regions.

The northern portion of the state, from a northeastern starting point along the state's border with Nevada and again moving westward toward the sea, consists mostly of sage-covered flatlands and hills giving way to pine-sheathed mountains and rolling, oak-covered hills.

California has forty-one peaks higher than 10,000 feet, the tallest being Mount Whitney at 14,496 feet. The Central Valley, totalling approximately one-fifth of the state's landmass, consists of farms and cultivated land and has little in the way of mineral values.

California can be divided into four basic types of terrain. These consist of coastal beaches, alpine mountain or oak-covered hills, inland deserts, and sage-covered flats. Along the 1,200 miles of coast, watchful beachcombers can find tide-washed jade, agate, abalone, and fossilized whale bone. Mountains and oaken-hill regions yield gold, clear and smoky quartz crystals, copper minerals, jade, serpentine, agate, petrified wood, and obsidian. Sage-flats and inland areas offer amethyst, obsidian, marble, agate, and fossils. Deserts, often the richest sources of collecting material, yield fossils, agate, geode, garnet, fire agate, jasper, copper minerals, gold, fluorite, translucent common opal, onyx, turquoise, and more!

Wintertime weather extremes range from below freezing in mountain and desert areas, to greater than 120 degrees Fahrenheit in the deserts during summer. Otherwise temperatures are generally moderate statewide. Rainfall can vary from 80 inches in northern coastal regions to nary a drop in the deserts. The mountains average 1 to 8 feet of snow depending on the location.

Coastal and inland foothills are covered with oak trees, wild oats, and, in the spring months, blanketed with California poppy, yellow mustard plant, and purple lupine. The mountains are forested with a variety of conifers and wild ferns, while blackberry brambles, poison oak, and poison ivy are found near creeks and streams. Desert vistas are adorned with the painful cholla cactus (sometimes called jumping cactus), beavertail and barrel cactus, wide expanses of creosote bush, ephedra (mormon tea), and mallow. Desert washes are silhouetted with mesquite trees, palo verde, and lavender gray smoke trees.

The geology of the state consists of some of the oldest rocks found in the world. Portions of the San Gabriel Mountain Range in southern California have been dated to 1.7 billion years old.

California's geologic variety is the result of an assortment of processes. Rocks forming the geology of the state have been the product of volcanic, sedimentary, and metamorphic mechanisms. Other ongoing processes continue to etch and chisel the landscape, such as weathering by wind and water. Cycles of drought, alternating with mud flows and landslides caused by prolific rainfall, wildfires, and earthquakes, continue to change and sculpt the landscape in dramatic ways. All have served to form and fashion California into a geologic wonderland. As a result of many dynamic processes, a great abundance of mineral and gem material awaits the eager rockhound.

The majority of rockhound collecting sites are on government lands managed by the Forest Service (USDAFS) or Bureau of Land Management (BLM). A few of these areas are designated as Wilderness Areas, which indicates that land use is severely limited to entry by foot or horseback. Areas so designated carry penalties for removal of any animal or plant species, as well as mineral or relic items. Although large tracts of land have been set aside as Wilderness Areas, a great many collecting areas abound throughout the state, offering the rockhound a smorgasbord of sites to choose from.

Earthquake Country

The Earth's outer mantle, called the lithosphere, is about 60 miles thick. The lithosphere is broken into approximately twelve great plates that ride upon a partially molten layer of rock called the asthenosphere. The plates move and flow slowly in different directions upon the asthenosphere. Plates may slide past one another, pull away from one another, or collide, usually with one plate subducting below the other. Subduction of one plate below another usually results in volcanic activity along the overriding plate, as happens in the northern section of California extending upward into Alaska. Mount Lassen, in northern California, is the southernmost active volcano along this type of subduction zone.

Two of the approximately twelve great plates, the Pacific and North American plates, meet and grind past each other in California, creating the right-lateral fault known as the San Andreas.

The San Andreas Fault cuts through the southern portion and partway into the northern portion of the state. The Pacific and North American plates slip past each another at an average rate of about two inches per year, causing minor to moderate earthquake activity along various segments of its length from time to time.

During the great San Francisco earthquake of 1906, the Pacific Plate slid an impressive and monumentally destructive 20 feet in a northward direction past the North American Plate.

Fault slippage, along the San Andreas and hundreds of other smaller faults, is the cause of much earthquake activity. Such slippage has made "California" synonymous with "earthquake." Yet it is only fair to remember that California is just one of thirty-nine other states in the Union which are known to have active earthquake faults.

Are earthquakes of major concern to mineral collectors and rockhounds visiting the state? No, of course not (says this native Californian). Although California is famous for earthquakes, very few actually occur on a day-to-day basis, and most are of such low magnitude as to be unnoticeable. Besides, the safest place to be during earthquakes is away from the cities and in the countryside, say for instance, on a rockhounding trip!

Sights to See

The geologic diversity of California makes for a great variety of must-see locations that have little to do with actual, in-the-field rockhounding, but everything to do with understanding and enjoying, not only basic geology, but the unique geology of California. Each of these places tells but a fraction of the story that is California.

Mitchell Caverns

Limestone caverns are a rarity in California. Why? Because limestone caverns are formed by two substances that California does not have in abundance, especially southern California where the Mitchell Caverns are located. These two rare substances are water and the carbonates from which limestone is formed. The fact that Mitchell Caverns exist in southern California makes them so unique.

Eons ago water percolated through the limestone of the Providence Mountains, dissolving cavities and tunnels, marking an ancient passage through the carbonate rock. The caverns lie in limestone wedged in by later intrusions of igneous rock. The caverns were formed millions of years ago when rainfall in the Mojave Desert was much greater than it is today. Dripping water, over eons, has dissolved the limestone, creating fantastic and fanciful shapes, forming columns and forests of tubular stalactites, stalagmites, and flow stone.

Two separate caves, Tecopa and El Pakiva, joined by a man-made tunnel, form the Mitchell Caverns. The interiors of the caverns are easy to negotiate since both have lighted walkways and stairs. Interesting features with names such as "The Bottomless Pit" and "The Queen's Chamber" intrigue visitors. Guided tours tell about the formation of the caves, as well as their history of habitation by both tribes people and desert creatures.

Year-round temperature within the caves is 65 degrees Fahrenheit, so a sweater or light jacket may be in order for the tour. Park personnel conduct tours from mid-September to mid-June, as desert summer temperatures outside the caverns become unbearably hot.

Self-guided tours include the nearby museum, housing a host of mineral specimens collected from the local mountains, and a nature walk, about a half-mile long. Signposts along the way will inform and enlighten visitors about the local plant and animal life. For further information and tour times call 619-389-2281. To get to Mitchell Caverns take Interstate 40 east from Barstow, located at the junction of I-40 and I-15. Drive 102 miles to Essex Road. Turn left (northwest) and follow Essex Road for 9.7 miles to Black Hills Road. Take the left fork 5.9 miles to the park's headquarters.

Death Valley

Death Valley has a magic all its own, and many have fallen under its spell. I know I have. As a result, I find myself making regular pilgrimages to imbibe the uncommon and severe beauty of its arid vistas. It has a rich and colorful history of mining, tragedy, and misadventure. More than a century ago intrepid adventurers entered Death Valley looking for gold, and many remained in the valley after their mines were worked out. Most famous of the mines is the Harmony Borax Works. Today in ruins, it can still be seen by visitors. Worked from 1882 to 1889, a mere seven years, it became famous for its twenty-mule-team-drawn wagons.

Furnace Creek, Badwater, Salt Creek, Dante's View, Devil's Golf Course and Hungry Bill's Ranch ruins are all interesting places to visit in Death Valley National Park. These name's are also descriptive of the types of experiences pioneers and early travelers had when visiting or passing through Death Valley. The austere and harsh conditions of blazing sun, little vegetation, scarce rain, devastating flash floods (when rain does occur), and wind erosion have created spectacular vistas that must be seen to be believed.

Death Valley is a place of extremes. Summer temperatures average 120 degrees Fahrenheit, with ground temperatures reaching 180 degrees, making Death Valley one of the hottest places in the world. Winter temperatures reach a low of 40 degrees, while fall, winter, and spring daytime temperatures average 60 to 70 degrees. These cooler seasons are the time to visit Death Valley. In spring visitors may be treated to colorful wildflower displays, usually after a winter of some rainfall in the surrounding mountains. Very little rain actually falls in the valley. Most moisture enters the valley periodically via flash floods roaring down from the surrounding mountains.

Much of the valley's elevation lies below sea level. The lowest point which is accessible by car is Badwater at 279.8 feet below sea level.

Other interesting places to see when visiting Death Valley are Scotty's Castle, a sprawling and richly appointed Spanish-Moorish-style mansion built by Albert Johnson, an insurance millionaire. The mansion cost $2.5 million to build many decades ago. Mr. Johnson had a friend named Walter Scott, a generally unsuccessful but picturesque prospector whose flamboyance, tall tales, and eccentricity made him a popular character in his day. The irrepressible Mr. Scott, or Scotty to those who knew him, was a frequent guest at the Death Valley mansion. With his flair and talent for prevarication, he managed to convince many listeners that the mansion was his own abode, purchased with the profits from his fabulous gold mine. This fabulous gold mine never really existed, except in Scotty's own vivid imagination, but he let slip subtle hints to avid listeners that it was located beneath "his" mansion.

Another interesting spot to visit in Death Valley is Ubehebe Crater, formed as the result of a violent, volcanic explosion thousands of years ago. The crater is 500 feet deep and one-half mile across. The landscape surrounding the crater is as barren and surreal as the surface of the moon.

The Racetrack is one of the most mysterious and intensely studied areas in the valley, by both scientists and mystics alike. The 2.5 mile, dry mudflat is the site of a little understood phenomenon. Here rocks, both large and small, seemingly move unaided across the flats, leaving faint trails behind them. The courses left by the rocks can be straight or curved, or even seem to double back upon themselves. No one has ever seen the rocks move nor captured it on film. Theories as to the cause range from extremely high winds to aliens!

I visited this mysterious area some years ago with my partners Mo and Ed Hemler. While theories regarding the rocks' movements have been postulated, another curious phenomenon of note has gone unmentioned. It is indeed a fact that many wild burros inhabit the area and leave their organic excretions all over the Racetrack. Curiously, this fecal detritus is also subject to the mysterious movement occurrences. However, the trails left by the burro droppings are often deeper and more apparent than those left by the heavier rocks. Here is a true mystery, one not as yet addressed—at least publicly—by the many experts who have studied and published theories on this mysterious movement phenomenon. I and my partners may one day return to Death Valley to attempt to solve this most unusual and, ummm, fertile of mysteries.

There are a variety of places to stay in Death Valley. There is the plush inn at Furnace Creek and the Furnace Creek Ranch, as well as Stove Pipe Wells Village. RVers will find dry camping as well as full hook-ups available. Tent campers have at least nine sites throughout the park to set up camp and stay awhile. Death Valley was designated a national park in 1995, therefore no mineral collecting is allowed within its borders. However, this guide lists several collecting sites outside Death Valley's boundaries.

When visiting Death Valley take extra drinking water. There are some services available, but these are few and far between. Stay out of mines. Frequently check your oil, fuel, and water temperature gauges. Keep tires at normal air pressure, as soft tires increase the chances of blowouts. If you have a breakdown, stay with your vehicle in the shade it provides. Park rangers patrol the paved roads on a regular basis. For more information, call 619-786-2331.

Natural History Museum of Los Angeles County

While there are many interesting and curious things to be seen here, rockhounds will find of particular interest the collections of dinosaurs and fossils. This museum also has an extensive mineral collection and one of the finest cut gemstone displays in the world. There is a fascinating collection of some of the fabulous and famous gold nuggets found during California's goldrush eras. There are also hands-on displays for children. The Natural History Museum is located at 900 Exposition Boulevard in Los Angeles. For more information call 213-744-3466.

George C. Page Museum of La Brea Discoveries

Also in Los Angeles, this museum, built over the La Brea Tar Pits, is the home and ongoing research center for saber-toothed cats, mammoths, wolves, and camels that were once native to the North American Continent and roamed throughout California. Many of these early mammals entered the tar pits looking for water and became mired, sinking to their deaths. There are fine displays of re-assembled skeletons and informative programs on these and other pre-historic plants and mammals. For more information call 213-936-2230.

California State Mining and Mineral Museum

This museum is located just off California 49 at the county fairgrounds near Mariposa in northern California. The mines near Mariposa were some of the richest in the Mother Lode. This museum displays more than 200,000 minerals, gems, and examples of Mother Lode gold. There is a hands-on mineral collection for kids, assay office, and stamp mill models. What makes this museum unusual is an actual gold mine tunnel, which visitors can enter and see life-size depictions of various mining scenes. Visitors can really get a taste of what gold mining was like at the turn of the century. This is the finest and largest museum in the Mother Lode country. For more information call 209-742-7625.

California Wildlife

While marine seals, sea otters, and a large variety of sea birds are encountered at beaches, other types of wildlife are most commonly found in the mountain and desert regions. Both these areas are home to North America's largest feral cat, the cougar, and that wily trickster, brother coyote. Black bears and deer range throughout mountain regions, while owls, rabbits, squirrels, and chipmunks are also frequently seen. Ospreys, condors, and eagles are less commonly observed.

Bighorn sheep roam some of the desert mountain areas but are elusive and rarely glimpsed. The only traces of their presence are usually cloven hoof prints in sandy desert washes, and these are often overlaid by the tracks of the desert cougar.

Look but don't touch! The California desert tortoise is protected by law.

The nasty cholla cactus, sometimes called a "jumping cactus," as the spines readily dislodge in clumps into passersby. The spines are barbed and painful to remove.

A wide variety of reptiles, from rattlesnakes, tortoises, and horny toads to Chuckwalla lizards, inhabit the desert regions. Common to the deserts of California is the packrat, the seed-packed middens of which can be found in nooks and crannies under rock overhangs. During twilight the engaging kangaroo rat may be seen hopping about on its long hind legs looking for a meal.

Deer, bobcats, and foxes also inhabit the deserts, their tracks evident around springs and natural seeps, which they visit during the early morning and early evening hours.

In springtime hairy tarantulas may be seen crossing dirt roads in the desert areas, while one-inch-diameter holes covered with gauzy webbing mark the hideouts of trap door spiders.

Mourning doves, hawks, crows, and quail are common throughout the state, along with many varieties of songbirds.

Desert Travel

While a little common sense suffices for mountain traveling, desert travel requires some know-how and plenty of caution.

First in importance is your vehicle. Your vehicle must be in good mechanical condition. Take extra belts and tools for minor repairs. Take plenty of water, several gallons for yourself and your group, and some for your vehicle should a radiator hose break. Take extra food in case of a breakdown. You could be waiting for several days before rescue arrives. During spring, fall, and winter warm days often turn into freezing nights. Bring warm clothes just in case. I like to dress in layers, then I can dress up or down, depending on the climatic conditions.

Tell someone where you are going and when you will return. Be specific and stick to your schedule.

Stay out of old mines. Rotten supports, rattlesnakes, vertical shafts, cave-ins, and poisonous gases are just some of the dangers awaiting those who attempt to explore old mines. The dangers of entering mines far outweigh any imagined riches or old relics one hopes to find. Remember, old mines have been abandoned *because* there is nothing more of value within.

The two reptiles to beware of are rattlesnakes and their deadlier cousin, the Mojave green, a rattlesnake mutation whose venom is a lethal neurotoxin. Look where you step and be careful not to place your hands into crevices that you cannot see into. This will prevent you from provoking rattlesnakes into biting. Rattlesnakes hibernate throughout the winter, emerging in March as the weather warms. However, it may be possible that rattlesnakes are unaware of this time schedule. They can emerge from hibernation early or late or even intermittently throughout the season, depending on weather conditions. Be cautious at all times.

California's Mineral Highlights

Gold is found throughout California, hence the name, "The Golden State." Although gold is found nearly everywhere in California, it is wise to keep in mind an old prospector's axiom: "Gold is where you find it, but it is not always found where you are looking!"

Serious prospecting for gold takes skill, a knowledge of geology and gold properties, and a few pieces of specialized equipment.

Gold panning, however, is an easy-to-learn activity in which many Californians indulge on weekends and vacations. They are often rewarded with grains and small nuggets. Panning for gold requires a gold pan, a small shovel, a pair of tweezers or tapered artist's paint brush—for picking gold flakes out of the gold pan—and a small, water-filled bottle in which to deposit the gold you find. Basically, gold panning consists of the shaking and agitation of water and gravel in the gold pan and the gentle sluicing off of the contents until all that remains is the heavier black sand. The black sand is swirled aside, and if you're lucky, you may see small flakes or even gold nuggets!

As gold would be an attractive addition to any rockhound's mineral collection, I have included one gold prospecting site for southern California and one for northern California.

Fire Agate

Fire agate, different than a regular agate, is actually a variety of microcrystalline quartz, or chalcedony. Fire agate forms in cracks, pockets, and fissures in rhyolite and basalt. Hydrothermal silica solutions seep into these crannies, where they cool and crystalize. Iron oxide in solution is laid down

A young prospector tries his luck on the gold-bearing San Gabriel River.

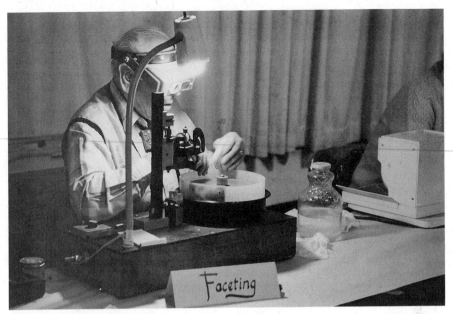

Rock and mineral clubs offer how-to demonstrations and lessons. Photo by W.R.C. Shedenhelm.

thinly between the layers of silica, creating multicolored fire. As additional layers of silica are deposited, botryoidal, or bubble-like forms, are created, which are typical of fire agate.

Vibrant iridescence, "fire," is often seen through these lens-like bubbles of chalcedony. The darker the fire agate, the more likely it is to contain fire.

Mining and removal of fire agate is best done by hand. When I dug fire agate at Opal Hill Mine in early 1994, very careful pick and chisel work were essential to keep from breaking or cracking the fire agate, which is softer than the surrounding rhyolite. It is often necessary to remove an entire pocket of surrounding material to retrieve the fire agate intact.

Patience and careful grinding and polishing will further reveal and enhance the fire within. However, the fire layer is so thin that the lapidary must be careful not to grind through it. Another problem encountered when working with fire agate is that the fire layers are not flat, but tend to pillow within the botryoidal bubbles. When working with fire agate, good lighting is recommended, as shadows deaden the fire and make it easy to overwork a piece. Frequently stopping to eyeball your piece helps to ensure you are not polishing away the fire. Patience and care are the keys here.

Fire agate may be worked using flex shaft equipment or regular cabbing equipment. It is usually worked into baroque designs in order to enhance and follow the natural iridescence and color patterns of the stone. Some success can be had using a rock tumbler, however, it is possible to lose some of the fire. A beautifully cut fire agate is a lovely and valuable gem that anyone would be proud to own or about which to say, "I found it!"

Benitoite

Benitoite is, so far, found only at one location, the Gem Mine in San Benito County. Its color varies from near colorless to intense blue. Its composition is barium-titanium-silicate. The crystals form in triangular-shaped pyramids and prisms and are found in association with white natrolite and black neptunite in hydrothermal replacement deposits.

Due to its relative hardness of 6.0 to 6.5, and lovely blue coloration, it is considered a gemstone. Due to its rarity, it is possible only to see benitoite in jewelry stores and museums.

Tourmaline

Tourmaline occurs in almost every color. The famous watermelon tourmaline has a pink center surrounded by a "rind" of green. Tourmaline is a prized gemstone, whatever its color. Its crystals are columnar in shape and striated lengthwise.

Tourmaline occurs in granite pegmatites with microcline, lepidolite, and spodumene. It is one of the mineral treasures of California and is found in the pegmatites of San Diego and Riverside counties. Tourmaline is a valuable and rare gemstone, and most of the tourmaline-bearing pegmatites are held by private claim.

Black tourmaline, or schorl, is a more common variety which can be found by rockhounds hunting unclaimed pegmatite deposits along Interstate 8 in southern California. Be sure that the pegmatites you are hunting are not claimed. Jewelry stores and museums are excellent places to view specimens of gem-grade tourmaline.

Clubs often put on annual shows where members and the public can buy and sell jewelry.
Photo by W.R.C. Shedenhelm.

Legends and Lore of Gems and Minerals

Studying geology and collecting rocks, gems, and minerals is a fascinating and satisfying endeavor in and of itself. However, no study is really complete unless we know something of the traditional aspect of our subject, in addition to our scientific examination. For rockhounds the study of geology often comprises both the historical and the scientific features of our hobby. The personal history of our hobby comes down to us in the form of the tradition and lore of the ancients.

To the ancients certain rocks, gems, and minerals had not only value as interesting collectibles or items of adornment, but perhaps more importantly, as talismans, amulets, and medicines. Even today in Chinese and Ayurvedic (Hindu) therapies, certain types of gems, minerals, and metals are used in infinitesimal amounts (often boiled with various herbs) for their curative and restorative properties. Even the trusted family doctor may use gold in therapeutic injections for the relief of arthritis pain.

Traditionally, stones were worn or carried as amulets or charms for protective or curative purposes, much as people today might wear a good-luck charm or religious medal. In ancient times a stone would often be inscribed with a magical symbol, glyph, or prayer to enhance the properties ascribed to it.

Therefore, it may be of interest to many collectors to learn of the traditional beliefs that were ascribed to by ancient civilizations, tribal peoples, healers, and alchemists.

Even today there are "New Age" beliefs concerning the curative powers of crystals and other stones, beliefs which have served to increase both the popularity and market value of many common stones—stones that rockhounds collect on a regular basis! The curative properties attributed to stones and minerals, be they imagined or real, will be debated for years among diverse groups. It is interesting to note that many retailers of minerals and gems have become knowledgeable in the lore of stones in order that they may better serve their customers.

The addition of information on the ancient lore and traditional beliefs concerning gems and minerals is intended to enhance and augment rockhounds' studies and knowledge of their hobby, while also introducing an interesting historical facet of the subject.

Rockhound's Vocabulary

Rockhounds, as do many other specialized groups, use various terms to describe rocks, minerals, terrain, or other aspects of their hobby. Many of these terms are confusing to beginners and may not be found in your Webster's Dictionary! Some terms are geologic jargon, while others have evolved through the processes of invention and usage, often catching on and becoming part of the rockhound's vocabulary. I have included some of the more common rockhound usages here.

Is this rock a "keeper" or a "leaverite" (see "Rockhound's Vocabulary")?

Geodes from Hauser geode beds.

Cab or cabochon: A smooth-polished gemstone, usually oval-shaped and with a domed top, but not always. Generally, it is cut, shaped, and polished but without facets.

Casts: A type of fossil form. Not all fossils are shells or bones. Some are imprints left after the original substance has worn away, leaving an impression or cavity where the original lay. This depression is called the "mold." Later when silt, silica, or other substances fill the mold, a cast is created.

Chalcedony: A variety of fine-grained, hard, massive (rather than crystallized) quartz. Its wide variety of colors, patterns, and varying degrees of translucence or opacity, as well as other elements in its make up, have given rise to a variety of names in attempts to describe it.

Even rockhounds do not always agree on the names. The word "agate" can be a catch-all term and is sometimes used interchangeably with any or all of the terms. Agate also describes a translucent form of chalcedony with banding. Carnelian often refers to a translucent yellow, orange, or red variety, which may also have banding. Bloodstone, or heliotrope, describes a green variety with red spots, or any other color with red spots for that matter. Moss agate is a chalcedony that is white or clear usually with dark, fern-like dendrites. Everyone pretty much agrees that chrysoprase is an apple green variety, while jasper is considered opaque and solid in color, has a variety of colors, or has a variegated or mottled pattern. Flint is found in shades of white, tan, gray, or black, but then so are agate and jasper.

Many rockhounds have very firm theories concerning this issue and will contest opposing theories with great vigor. As stated, these rules are not cast in concrete nor agreed upon even by rockhounds. Even I, while fairly firm on some of the terms, still swap the terms jasper, chalcedony, and agate, as well as carnelian, sard, and sardonyx, with fairly free abandon. Hopefully this list, if it provides nothing else, will serve to give novice rockhounds an idea of what they are in for when talking "agate" with old-timers.

Cleavage: The way minerals split along molecular planes, usually parallel to crystal faces, serving to identify many rocks and minerals.

Color: Often used as an identifying feature. However, color may be due to impurities within the sample and is not always a useful identifying property.

Country rock: The prevailing geology of an area that surrounds a vein or pocket of lode or gem material.

Crystal form: Also called crystallography. Crystals form with a variety of faces based on their molecular structure. The placement, number, and shape of the crystal faces are identifying features.

Cutting material: Usually indicates rock or gem elements that are hard enough and dense enough for use in jewelry, sculpture, or other lapidary projects.

Dendrites: Fern-like inclusions in a mineral usually of manganese or pyrolusite.

Desert varnish: A black or brown coating on rocks found in the desert usually as a result of iron or manganese oxides.

Druse or drusy: A term used to describe a crust of tiny quartz crystals.

Float: Material which has eroded away or fallen from a mineral deposit and is often used by rockhounds to track a mineral back uphill to its source.

Fracture: The broken surface of a mineral. Non-crystalline rock forms often break along fracture lines, rather than cleavage planes.

Hardness: One of several methods used to identify an unknown rock (see Mohs scale).

Igneous: Refers to rocks or geologic formations that are a direct result or product of volcanism or deep-seated plutonics. Examples: basalt and granite.

Keeper: A slang term used to denote rock that is too good to throw away or leave behind.

Lapidary: The art of cutting or polishing stones or one who engages in the art.

Leaverite: Another slang term which means the opposite of "keeper." New rockhounds will often inquire of the senior rockhounds what this term "leaverite" means. The neophyte will then be informed, "It's no good. So leave 'er right there!"

Luster: The way in which a mineral absorbs or reflects light, a useful identifying factor. Luster is classified usually as dull, earthy, silky, greasy, pearly, resinous, vitreous (glass-like), or adamantine (diamond-like).

Malpai: A flat area, devoid of vegetation, most often found in the desert. The area looks like a manmade pavement, although it is natural. The "pavement" consists of desert-varnished rock. It is also often referred to as "desert pavement."

Metamorphic: Rocks that have been changed, usually by heat, pressure, or permeation, by other substances. These changes often result in an alteration of the basic crystalline structure of the rock, as well as its appearance. Examples: gneiss, slate, marble.

Mohs scale: The graduated, relative hardness of rocks on a scale from one to ten. One is the softest and ten is hardest.

1. Talc	6. Orthoclase
2. Gypsum	7. Quartz
3. Calcite	8. Topaz
4. Fluorite	9. Corundum
5. Apatite	10. Diamond

This scale is useful to rockhounds and collectors when trying to identify an unknown rock or mineral. Some common materials display a hardness factor that can be used to help determine the identity of a rock specimen, even if one does not have all the minerals of the Mohs scale. A fingernail has a hardness of 2.5, a penny has a hardness of 3, a piece of glass or a knife blade has a hardness of 5.5, and steel has a hardness of 6.5. The hardness of a rock is determined by scratching your unknown specimen upon other rocks or substances of known hardness and then scratching these on your specimen. Harder rocks will scratch softer ones, while softer ones usually leave a powder trail on the harder rocks. Through this procedure the hardness of the rock in question may be determined.

Sedimentary: Rocks which are formed by sediments of sand, silt, or mud and have become compacted and hard. Sedimentary rocks are often characterized by layering. Examples: sandstone, shale, conglomerate.

Streak: The true color a mineral makes when rubbed against a piece of unglazed porcelain. This is often different than the apparent color of a mineral and is a better identifying feature. This is particularly true of the metallic ores where color and streak may be different due to impurities or oxidation.

Rockhound Rules

As mentioned above, I have been chastised by my use of "free-association" of terms regarding the various types of chalcedony. However, I have a theory: It is more important how one collects a rock, than what one calls it.

So here is a brief listing of what I consider important rules for rockhounds of all ages, not necessarily in order of importance.

1. Do not throw rocks. This one applies to all ages for a variety of important reasons.

2. Do not litter. This rule is important if rockhounds want to continue to be welcomed at collecting sites. Marking areas with graffiti or defacing petroglyphs, pictographs, or intaglios are also considered littering and vandalism.

Proper technique for opening fossil trilobites. Note goggles for eye safety.

3. Stay between the lines. This means sticking to established roads and jeep trails. Not only does driving off established routes mark up the landscape and destroy vegetation, it also unnecessarily interferes with wildlife. In a desert environment especially, tire tracks only take moments to create and can remain for decades. If we are to maintain access to collecting areas, we must police ourselves. Fortunately for rockhounds, there are roads and jeep trails leading to our collecting areas. We do not have to stray from between the lines.

4. Do not trespass. Obey all "no-trespassing, "do-not-enter," or "keep-out" signs and those stating private mineral claims. Not only is this a safety precaution, but it respects the rights of property owners and claim holders. If you wish to collect on private property, always obtain permission first.

5. Be prepared. Go on your trips adequately prepared to administer first-aid to yourself, your family and friends, and your vehicle. Take into consideration the weather, terrain, and other conditions you may encounter. Pack and plan accordingly.

6. Do not be greedy. Pick up only what you can use or display, leaving some for others, or yourself, to collect should you return someday.

7. Be kind to animals. Many creatures are on the endangered species list. Gone are the days when you could take home a desert tortoise as a pet. They are an endangered species.

Most rockhounds automatically act in environmentally responsible and respectful ways when out in the wilderness. Rockhounding is an environmentally, low-impact form of recreation.

So what are some of the things rockhounds are allowed to do when pursuing their hobby?

1. You may bend over, stoop, squat, crawl, or grovel in your efforts to find the perfect rock. Remember in rockhounding no posture or position used to find a rock is considered too ignoble.

2. You may pick up a rock merely because you like it, whether or not anyone else approves. The selection of a rock or mineral is a highly personal matter.

3. You may dampen your rock to see what its true colors and patterns are. There are a variety of ways to do this. The extremely fastidious use a squirt bottle. The semi-fastidious (like me) lick them. And the old-timers spit on them.

4. You may take the kids. The more kids the better. Not only are kids natural rockhounds, they always seem to know where the really good rocks are hiding. Besides, there is nothing like the natural wonder of a child to re-instill in adults a sense of wonder.

5. You may take home only the best of what you find. Rocks take up lots of room. Before long your garage, yard, and home will be like mine, overflowing with them.

Rocks are beautiful. There are hundreds of things you can do or make with your rocks. They also look great just sitting on a shelf or window sill. Visitors to my house always pick them up and admire them. Sometimes I give them to my guests, if they don't want to part with my rocks. They make great gifts, and they are wonderful items to share with classmates during "show and tell" at school. They are also good for trading and swapping for other good stuff.

How To Use This Guide

The sites in this guide are divided into three sections: **Rockhounding Sites in Southern California, Rockhounding Sites in Coastal California,** and **Rockhounding Sites in Northern California.**

Maps are very important for finding collecting sites. Where possible, I have included information on other maps, such as U.S. Geological Survey (USGS) maps, USDAFS maps, or BLM maps, that cover the sites listed in this guide. These maps cover a wider area and show more details, such as geographical contours, buildings, springs, or other places that might be of interest to rockhounds.

Maps are essential for finding collecting sites, especially in the desert.

When collecting in the desert, you will find many dirt roads that are not shown on any maps. New roads have been created by recreational, off-road vehicles. Therefore, mileage and directional heading become essential when attempting to choose between several dirt roads in order to get to your chosen collecting area.

In using maps to find locations, especially in the desert, it is helpful to have a directional compass along. Most compasses are affected by the electrical systems in automobiles and will not work properly inside a vehicle. Automotive stores sell compasses that can be set to disregard the electrical systems of automobiles. They are generally reasonable in cost and well worth the time and small effort required to install.

USGS maps may be purchased at most sporting goods stores, cartography shops, or ordered by writing or calling the Geological Survey division of the United States Department of the Interior and requesting their catalog. To get a copy of their catalog write to: Geological Survey, Box 25286, Federal Center, Denver, Colorado 80225, or call 303-236-7477. The waiting period for receiving ordered maps is usually a couple of months, so order well in advance of your need. The advantage to ordering maps directly from the USGS is that it is still possible to order some 15-minute maps, which are no longer printed and have become unavailable for purchase in most stores. They also cost less when ordered from their source.

Most map shops sell only the 7.5-minute maps, and you must purchase several of these—each one costing the same as a single 15-minute map—in order to cover the same area normally depicted on a single 15-minute map. However, to make locating the sites listed in this book simpler, all references to USGS maps will refer to 7.5-minute series.

You may order BLM's Desert Access guides for Southern California by calling 909-697-5200. Ordering maps over the phone is simplified by use of a major credit card. Maps are mailed immediately and will usually arrive only two or three days later. USDAFS maps may be purchased at Forest Service ranger stations.

Mileage has been given with all site maps in this guide. It is important to realize that mileage may vary up to 0.2 miles from one vehicle to another.

Most collecting sites listed in this guide will be located on public lands managed by the USDAFS or BLM. Most of the fee sites are located on land that is under valid mining or mineral claims or may be on patented claims. A patented claim is one where the government has deeded all rights and ownership of the land to the claimant.

When collecting rocks and minerals in California, it is important to be aware of the possibility that land status is subject to change. Mining claims may be filed that overlay known rockhound collecting sites or on-going legislation may create new Wilderness Areas that encompass old collecting sites, making it illegal to remove anything from them. When rockhounding in California, obey all signs regarding current land status and respect all claim markers and no-trespassing signs. Above all be safe, have fun. And good rockhounding to you!

Rockhound Access to Commercial Mines

The famous tourmaline group of mines at Pala near San Diego are no longer open to rockhounds for collecting. They do not anticipate reopening for collecting by the public in the near future. If you would like to see or purchase lovely examples of tourmaline from these famous mines, you may visit The Collector, their museum/shop located at 912 S. Live Oak Park Road, Fallbrook, CA 92028, or call 619-728-9121.

One weekend a year, usually in October, the company that mines the mineral-rich Searles Lake near Trona opens certain sections up to rockhound collecting. For current dates and other information, contact the local gem and mineral club shown in the club listings.

Similarly, U.S. Borax opens their mine periodically to collectors. Check with the offices of U.S. Borax at Boron or Los Angeles for current dates, times, and restrictions.

SITE 1 *FIRE AGATE AT OPAL HILL MINE*

Land type: Desert mountains.
Best season: November to April.
Tools: Sledge, pick, chisels, gads, whisk broom.
Material: Fire agate, dog-tooth calcite crystals, gypsum, fluorite, quartz crystals, clinoptilolite.
Lore: Native American and Mexican beliefs hold that fire agate enhances tissue regeneration and energizes psychic centers.
Special attraction: Wiley Well, a watering station for the historic Bradshaw Stage Trail.
Elevation: 1,200 feet.,
Land manager: Private claim.
Vehicle type: 4X4 from Wiley Well. Two-wheel-drive vehicle from Palo Verde.
For more information: Nancy Hill-Fisher, c/o Opal Hill Mine, P.O. Box 497, Palo Verde, CA 92666.
Finding the site: To get to the mine four-wheel-drive vehicles may exit Interstate 10 at Wiley Well. Wiley Well Road is well-graded and maintained by the Bureau of Land Management. However, only four-wheel-drive vehicles should attempt the 1.9-mile drive to the mine from Wiley Well Road. Two-wheel-drive vehicles should enter from the town of Palo Verde. Take the Fourth Street exit from California 78 and follow the signs 9 miles to the mine. Camping is available at Wiley Well and Coon Hollow campgrounds and on the flats along the road from Palo Verde.

Rockhounding: Opal Hill Mine is the only site in California where high-quality fire agate is found. The Opal Hill fire agate is well known for its brilliant, cherry red fire. However, iridescent greens (my favorite), yellows, oranges, and blues are commonly found as well. Of interest to micromount collectors, fine specimens of tiny quartz crystal clusters and crystalline flowers can also be found.

As of last year, amygdules containing crystals and nodules of fire agate have been unearthed. These are considered rare and very valuable if dug intact. As digging goes ever deeper into the mountain, a greater variety of minerals and collectibles continues to be disclosed.

Many rockhounds may remember the mine's former owner, an irascible and cantankerous woman known for her prickly manner and salty language that was well-peppered with expletives. She was also renowned, in Palo Verde, for driving her bulldozer into the town for a late-night binge at the local saloon. The mine has been under new management for more than eight years.

Nancy Hill-Fisher is owner and operator of the Opal Hill Mine. Her husband, Howard, assists in management. Nancy and Howard will help visitors locate and dig quality fire agate. Along with a three- or four-pound sledge

SITE 1 *FIRE AGATE AT OPAL HILL MINE*
SITE 2 *PEBBLE TERRACE*

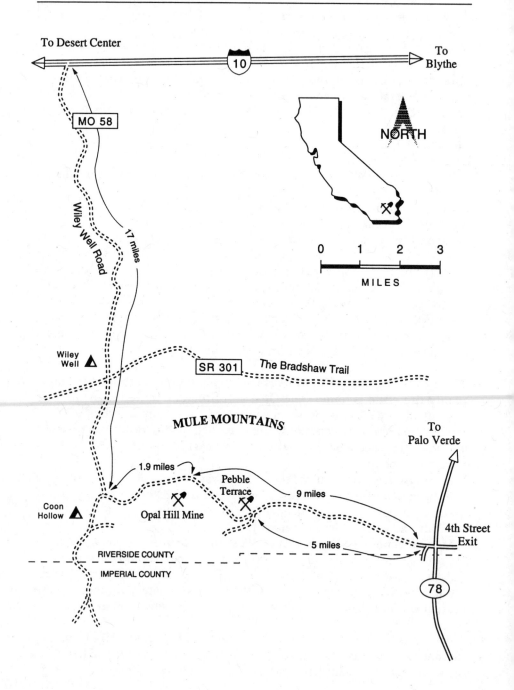

To Desert Center

To Blythe

10

MO 58

NORTH

0 1 2 3

MILES

Wiley Well Road

17 miles

Wiley Well ▲

SR 301 The Bradshaw Trail

MULE MOUNTAINS

To Palo Verde

1.9 miles

Pebble Terrace

9 miles

Coon Hollow ▲

Opal Hill Mine

4th Street Exit

5 miles

RIVERSIDE COUNTY

IMPERIAL COUNTY

78

Nancy Hill-Fisher, mine owner, unearths a "keeper!" (A nice specimen of fire agate).

Polished fire agate from Opal Hill.

hammer, rock pick, gad bar, and chisel, a whisk broom is essential for sweeping aside dirt so that you can see when you've uncovered a nice piece of fire agate.

Specimens of fire agate also can be found by walking about with eyes glued to the ground. For those who prefer to acquire their fire agate with no exertion whatsoever, nicely finished and polished pieces are sold at the mine for very reasonable prices.

Digging fees are subject to change, but early in 1994 the fee was fifteen dollars per day per person, with a special rate for couples, groups, and seniors. Kids are especially welcome and dig for free. For those planning to spend several days digging, a few small trailers are available to overnight in. These overnight accommodations were available at no extra cost, however, this may be subject to change. Meals are not included, so bring your own food and beverages.

SITE 2 *PEBBLE TERRACE*

Land type: Desert.
Best season: October to April.
Tools: Rock pick, collecting bag.
Material: Multi-colored moss, plume agates.
Lore: Romans and Greeks used agate for protection and courage, while moss agate enhanced positive emotions.
Special attraction: Opal Hill Fire Agate Mine.
Elevation: 980 feet.
Land manager: BLM.
Vehicle type: Any.
For more information: USGS map Thumb Peak Quadrangle; BLM's Desert Access Guide Midway Well #21. See map on p. 24.
Finding the site: From Palo Verde take the Fourth Street exit from California 78. Drive 5 miles to Pebble Terrace. You will see a sign that points the way to the Opal Hill Mine and informs you that you have reached Pebble Terrace. The sign also informs that no commercial collecting is allowed. However, individuals and groups of rockhounds are welcome.

Rockhounding: This is a well-known site which was favored by rockhounds from the 1930s and well into 1960s. Consequently, the concern was that it might be over-collected, with little interest to the rockhound remaining. This is not the case. The area still has abundant material, it's just hard to see! Desert varnish covers all the rounded agates, shaped by water. This area was once underwater eons ago, and water action has left the area looking like the tide went out and never returned. This area is under appreciated today by rockhounds merely because it looks like nothing is here except a bunch of black cobbles of varying sizes.

The technique for hunting this area was shown to me by Herman Schob of Cathedral City. Pick up any rock and strike a glancing blow with your rock pick. This will dislodge a flake of the outer discolored skin and reveal the true color of the agate within. There are agates of bland and uninteresting color, but there are also treasures hiding under the desert varnish.

Hunting Pebble Terrace was like an Easter egg hunt. One never knows what might be camouflaged at one's feet. I found several beautifully colored and patterned agates. My prize was a palm-size, cream-colored moss agate with green moss-like inclusions.

SITE 3 BLACK AND PAISLEY AGATE

Land type: Desert hills.
Best season: October to May.
Tools: Rock pick, bag, chisel.
Material: Black agate, lavender and green paisley agate, pink and cream-banded agate.
Lore: Greeks and Romans wore agate for protection and to inspire courage.
Special attractions: Thumb Peak and Clapp Spring.
Elevation: 820 feet.
Land manager: BLM.
Vehicle type: Two-wheel-drive truck.
For more information: USGS map Thumb Peak Quadrangle.
Finding the site: From Wiley Well drive 5.6 miles south to an unmarked road to your left, heading east. Follow this road 1.3 miles. Do not take the road to the left. From this point continue 0.3 miles and stop. There are seams of black agate on the low slopes to your left. Drive another 0.3 miles and stop. Again on the slopes to your left is a location known for its lavender and green paisley agate.

Rockhounding: The black agate will require some pick and chisel work to remove. However, when I visited in early 1994, some kind soul had done the chisel work, and all I had to do was pick it up and bag it. Some black agate, as float, will be covered with desert varnish. A glancing blow with your rock pick on the edge of the stone will chip off a section revealing the color within. Most of the float is a dull gray inside and of little interest to rockhounds.

The paisley agate was in short supply upon my recent visit, however, I found fair amounts of a lovely pink and cream-banded agate reminiscent of wonderstone on the left slopes and also in the area to the right of the road.

The pink and cream agate made my visit well worth while. It would make beautiful cabochons for rings, small belt buckles, bolas, and brooches. Most pieces were palm-sized or smaller.

At first glance it may be difficult for rockhounds to identify the pink agate from the surrounding float, as it too is covered with desert varnish. Looking closely will reveal that the pink agate, still coated with desert varnish, is glossy, while the surrounding rocks are a dull, matte finish.

If you return to the left fork at 1.3 miles and take that road another 0.2 miles, you will have a fine view of Thumb Peak with its unique configuration. From here on to Clapp Spring a 4X4 will be necessary. Another 0.2 miles will bring you to a fork in the road, veer left. For the next 3.1 miles ignore all roads to the left, and you will arrive at Clapp Spring after crossing several sandy washes. The site is marked by several California fan palms. The spring was used by Indians and later by cattlemen to water their herds by piping water from the spring into watering troughs. The nearby caves were used by Indian hunting parties.

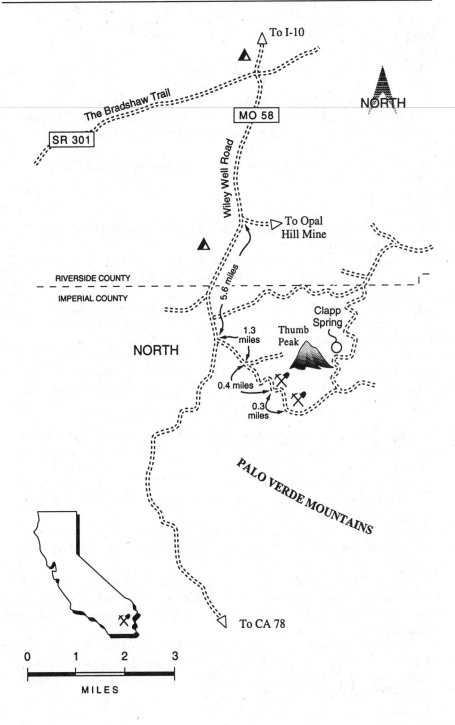

SITE 4 *CRYSTAL-FILLED AMYGDULES*

Land type: Desert.

Best season: October to May.

Tools: Rock pick, bag.

Material: Crystal- and zeolite-filled amygdules, chalcedony roses, calcite rhombs.

Lore: Greeks and Romans wore chalcedony to heighten peaceful, calm feelings and for protection while traveling or as a shield against negative energy. Europeans wore chalcedony for success in lawsuits and to increase lactation.

Special attraction: General Patton's World War II training field.

Elevation: 700 feet.

Land manager: BLM.

Vehicle type: 4X4.

For more information: USGS maps Little Chuckwalla Mountains and east of Aztec Mines quadrangles.

Finding the site: From Interstate 10 heading west from Blythe, take the Ford Dry Lake offramp onto Chuckwalla Valley Road. Head west for 2.8 miles to Graham Pass. It will be marked with a vertical white post topped with an old whiskey bottle. From the east take Interstate 10 and exit at Corn Springs onto Chuckwalla Valley Road. Head southeast for 13.2 miles to Graham Pass. Drive in a southerly direction on Graham Pass for a total of 9.1 miles (The road, as indicated on the map at 5.9 miles, is difficult to see from Graham Pass). At 9.1 miles turn left and drive 2 miles to the amygdule site. In getting to the amygdule site, a 4X4 vehicle may be needed to negotiate a twisting, turning drive through a large wash.

Rockhounding: The amygdule deposit is to the left of the road at the two-mile mark and descends down into the wash. The amygdules are lima bean-size to fist-size and contain a variety of crystals, mostly miniature, clear quartz crystals. More rare, but worth looking for, some contain crystals of the zeolite group of minerals. These tiny quartz and zeolite crystals will delight the hearts of micromount collectors.

Most of the amygdules are loose in decomposed volcanic rock and are very plentiful. A few are still embedded, although easily removed with a rock pick.

Also in the area chalcedony roses are found. The roses are well-formed and whether merely cleaned up or tumble polished, make lovely jewelry pins. They look especially elegant containing a pearl or surrounding polished coral or a black agate piece.

Calcite rhombs are found by looking on the sides of the road. The calcite deposits are easy to spot; they look like circular patches of snow against the dark, desert pavement. Some of the calcite is crystallized in the interesting rhombohedral form common to calcite.

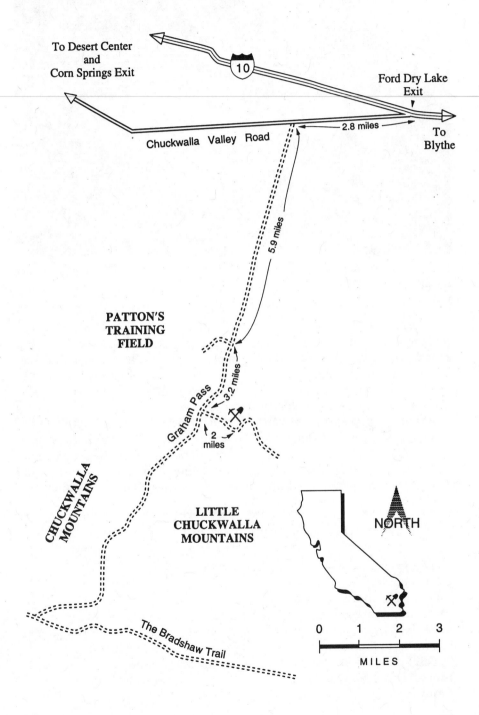

To Desert Center
and
Corn Springs Exit

Ford Dry Lake
Exit

To
Blythe

2.8 miles

Chuckwalla Valley Road

5.9 miles

PATTON'S
TRAINING
FIELD

Graham Pass

3.2 miles

2
miles

CHUCKWALLA
MOUNTAINS

LITTLE
CHUCKWALLA
MOUNTAINS

The Bradshaw Trail

NORTH

0   1   2   3
MILES

Chalcedony amygdule filled with translucent agate with cavity lined with drusy quartz crystals.

Whether gently broken with a tap of the rock pick, sliced, or cut in half, the amygdules reveal their crystalline interiors and make interesting jewelry and specimen pieces. Tumble polishing smooths and shines the chalcedony exterior of the amygdules. It reduces their thickness and reveals crystal points that shimmer and glitter beneath a thin skin of translucent chalcedony, catching the light in interesting ways.

At about 5 miles from the start of Graham Pass onward, on both sides of the road, is General Patton's World War II training field. Tank tracks may still be seen on the desert pavement. A friend of mine recently found an old olive-drab flashlight and a sterling silver compass in this area. Interesting artifacts can be found especially in or near washes after heavy rains.

SITE 5 *HAUSER GEODE BEDS*

Land type: Desert hills.
Best season: October to April.
Tools: Pick, shovel, rock bag.
Material: Agate and crystal-filled geodes, red and green agate.
Lore: In Europe, geodes were believed to be the abode of elemental spirits and were related to female energy due to egg-like shapes.
Special attraction: The historic Bradshaw Stage Trail.
Elevation: 1,150 feet.
Land manager: BLM.

SITE 5 *HAUSER GEODE BEDS*

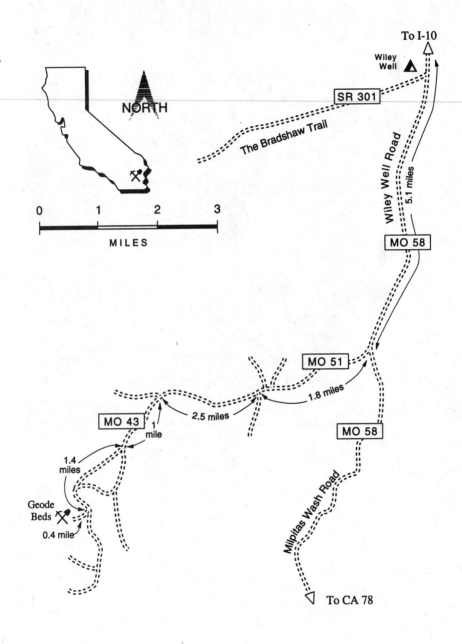

To I-10

Wiley Well

SR 301

The Bradshaw Trail

NORTH

0   1   2   3

MILES

Wiley Well Road

5.1 miles

MO 58

MO 51

1.8 miles

2.5 miles

MO 43

1 mile

1.4 miles

MO 58

Geode Beds

0.4 mile

Milpitas Wash Road

To CA 78

Herman Schob of Cathedral City digs geodes at the Hauser Beds.

Vehicle type: Any.

For more information: USGS map Wiley Well Quadrangle; BLM's Desert Access Guide Midway Well #21.

Finding the site: This is an extremely difficult site to find. So chronological mileage has been included following the "Finding the site" information. From Wiley Well drive south 5.1 miles on Wiley Well Road (M058) to a road leading to the right. Drive in a westerly direction for 1.8 miles. At this point you will veer right, go through a shallow wash, and continue for another 2.5 miles where you will take the road to your left that should be marked as M043. Stay to the left for 1 mile, avoiding a road to the right after 0.2 of a mile.

At the one-mile mark take the road to your right and continue for 1.4 miles, staying on the well-marked road. At the 1.4-mile mark take the road to the right and continue 0.4 miles to a campfire ring near a large gully. Park and walk down into and back up the other side of this gully. Continue walking.

When you come up out of the second gully you find yourself on or near a narrow footpath to the left. Follow this footpath down through another gully. You'll lose the footpath where it rejoins the road through the gullies. As you walk, you will see a shallow wash to your left. Cross a shallow gully. Geodes have been dug all along this wash. Continue walking until a footpath heads directly to the wash at a shallow point. The walk is about one-quarter mile. This is the area where Herman Schob and I dug plenty of geodes in the late winter of 1994. Start digging where the ashy embankment is still intact at the far edge of the wash. The geodes will fall out as you dig.

Chronological mileage log: From Wiley Well drive south on Wiley Well Road for 5.1 miles. Turn onto the road to your right. Set your mileage indicator to zero. You will not reset your indicator during the drive to the site. Drive 1.8 miles in a westerly direction. Veer right through a shallow wash and continue. At 4.3 miles take the left fork (M043). Stay to your left at 4.5 miles. At 5.3 miles take the fork to your right. At 6.3 you will dip through a shallow wash. At 6.6 miles stay to your left, keeping to the well-marked road. At 6.7 take the road to your right. At 7.1 park near the campfire ring and continue as above.

Rockhounding: The Hauser Geode Beds are very difficult to find due to an interlacing of numerous roads. However, almost all roads in this area lead to numerous geode beds, and unfortunately most have been completely dug out over the years. I have encountered many people driving about in this area looking for the beds, but never finding the one they intended to visit or being sure if they had arrived at the one they wanted to search. The part of the Hauser Beds listed in this site is relatively unknown, at present.

The ashy embankment is soft and easily broken apart with a small pick or folding shovel. The best method is to scrape away the bank one layer at a time, picking out the fist-size geodes as they fall out. We uncovered many geodes in the shallow wash where you see signs of digging at the farthest

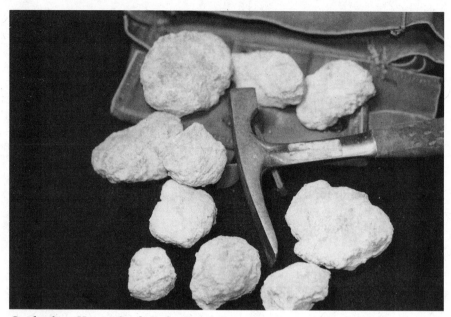

Geodes from Hauser Geode Beds.

point. Most have solid agate interiors displaying mottled markings in white, clear, beige, gray, chocolate, and a lovely pastel salmon. Some of the geodes contain a solid, translucent, agate interior with bands and streaks of white. One lovely double geode that I found contained a cavity with perfect, clear, quartz crystals massed inside.

On the narrow footpath leading out of the second gully, nice chunks of red and green agate can be picked up. Seams of this agate weather out from above on the mountains and roll down onto the path.

SITE 6 *PSILOMELANE NEAR WILEY WELL*

Land type: Desert mountain.
Best season: October to April.
Tools: Rock pick, collecting bag.
Material: Botryoidal psilomelane.
Lore: New Age beliefs maintain that psilomelane, worn or carried, enhances psychic vision and development.
Special attraction: Stone fortifications below psilomelane diggings.
Elevation: 820 feet.
Land manager: BLM.
Vehicle type: Any.
For more information: USGS map Wiley Well; BLM's Desert Guide Midway Well #21.

SITE 6 *PSILOMELANE NEAR WILEY WELL*

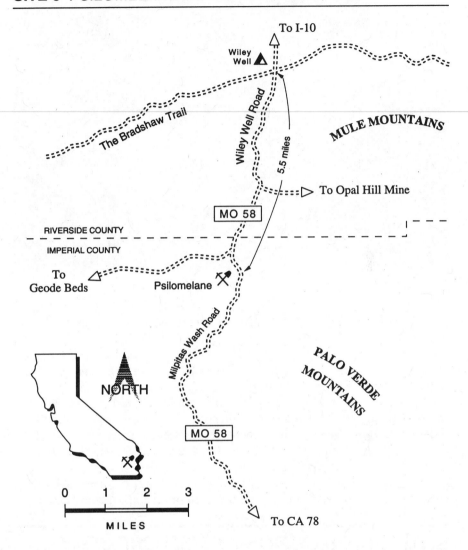

Finding the site: From Wiley Well drive south on Wiley Well Road (it changes names to Milpitas Wash Road at the Imperial County line) 5.5 miles to some low mountains to the right of the road. Pull off onto the flat area to your right. Walk up the side of the nearest low mountain to the signs of digging at the top.

Rockhounding: Though smaller in area than the Arlington Mine Site, this site is just off Wiley Well Road and easy to get to if you don't mind a little walk up the side of a low mountain. It is also convenient if visiting the other sites in the Wiley Well/ Bradshaw Trail area. Good botryoidal and semi-

37

Botryoidal psilomelane near Wiley Well.

metallic cutting material is plentiful, as are nice velvety specimen pieces.

The stone fortifications, easily seen from Wiley Well Road, are interesting to see on your way up the mountain. A low stone wall has been erected along the flank of the mountain, and above that are several circular constructions. Opinions vary as to the purpose of these structures. Some speculate that they were built by prehistoric tribes people as wind breaks. Possibly the structures were erected during wartime training as fortifications, although no ration cans or other recent debris is evident.

The desert varnish pebbles, which litter the area between the mountain and the road, are worth chipping with a rock pick in order to reveal their interior color. Some are lovely agates that would make colorful cabochons. However, be prepared to chip quite a few in order to find some keepers.

SITE 7 *CHALCEDONY ROSE GARDEN AND GROSSULAR CRYSTALS AT AUGUSTINE PASS*

Land type: Desert hills.
Best season: October to April.
Tools: Rock pick, collecting bag.
Material: Chalcedony roses, grossular crystals.
Lore: Greeks and Romans believed that chalcedony, worn or carried, protected travelers and prevented nightmares. Early Egyptians and European

SITE 7 CHALCEDONY ROSE GARDEN AND GROSSULAR CRYSTALS AT AUGUSTINE PASS

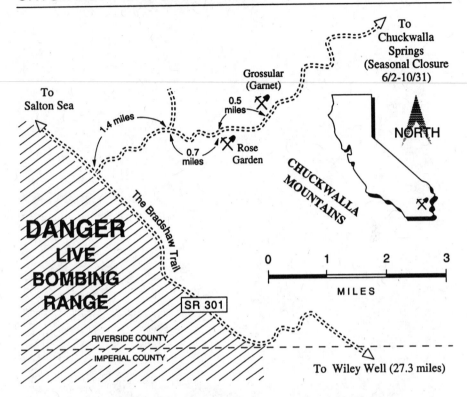

alchemists held that clear grossular (a type of garnet) energized the pineal gland located in the brain. It was also used to protect against crime, to cure inflammation, aid the bloodstream, and strengthen the skeletal system.

Special attraction: Augustine Pass.

Elevation: 2,300 feet.

Land manager: BLM.

Vehicle type: 4X4, dune buggy.

For more information: USGS maps Augustine Pass and Chuckwalla Spring quadrangles; BLM's Desert Access Guide Salton Sea #20.

Finding the site: From Wiley Well drive 0.2 miles south to the Bradshaw Trail. Turn right or southwest on the Bradshaw Trail. DO NOT GO SOUTH OF THE BRADSHAW TRAIL. THIS AREA IS A LIVE AERIAL BOMBING RANGE. Drive 27.3 miles to a road to your right marked with a rusted, hole-ridden water tank. Take this road, and at 1.4 miles bear right (east by northeast). Continue 0.7 miles and park to the right at the foot of the hill. There is room here for several cars to pull off the road and park. The area is marked by a stone campfire ring. The mountain to the right is covered with chalcedony roses.

Grossular (garnet) crystals from Augustine Pass.

A shovel marks the dark rodingite vein carrying grossular crystals in Augustine Pass.

Rockhounding: To find the chalcedony roses, walk up and all around the mountain. You will see them littering the mountainside. The roses start out as oddly-shaped, thin-skinned nodules. As you walk about the mountain, you will find the seams from which they erode. The nodules break as they weather out, which results in the classical lacy-shaped roses. Some are covered with white to buff drusy quartz that sparkle in the sun. All make nice jewelry pieces with cleaning and a little polishing of the edges. The roses may also be tumble polished.

If you drive another 0.5 miles over Augustine Pass, you will enter a deep, narrow wash. This is one of several rodingite contact zones where I was able to remove nice pockets of grossular crystals using crack-hammers, sledges, gads, and chisels. Most of the crystals recovered were crystal clear. Some were clear with chocolate matrices and more rare were hessonite, which are orangish red in color. The rodingite contact zones show as green and red belts in otherwise grayish country rock.

In early 1994 only a smattering of tiny crystals were visible on the rodingite contact at 0.5 miles. However, testing with a rock pick revealed several hollow-sounding areas that could be possible crystal pockets. Hard work is the only way to find out. Rodingite contacts occur in various places throughout the length of the pass.

Augustine Pass has been the site of considerable mining, most likely for gold, from the late 1800s through 1930. Mining relics are to be found throughout the pass. In 1905 a bleached skeleton was found at the pass, a rusted gold pan and a pocket watch nearby. Only short-base 4X4s are recommended for attempting to drive through the pass to Chuckwalla Springs. This is a seasonal route. It is closed from June 2 through October 31.

SITE 8 *CHUCKWALLA WELL AGATE AND JASPER*

Land type: Desert hills.
Best season: November to April.
Tools: Rock pick, collecting bag.
Material: Agate, jasper.
Lore: Agate and jasper were worn by the ancients for protection and courage. Jasper was believed to have rain-bringing qualities.
Special attraction: Bradshaw Trail explorations.
Elevation: 2,100 feet.
Land manager: BLM.
Vehicle type: 4X4.
For more information: USGS map Chuckwalla Spring Quadrangle.
Finding the site: From Chuckwalla Valley Road take Graham Pass Road approximately 17 miles south to the Bradshaw Trail. Head west (right) on the Bradshaw Trail for 3.4 miles. Turn right onto a road and drive an additional 0.5 miles. Search the hills that rise up behind the well area.

SITE 8 *CHUCKWALLA WELL AGATE AND JASPER*

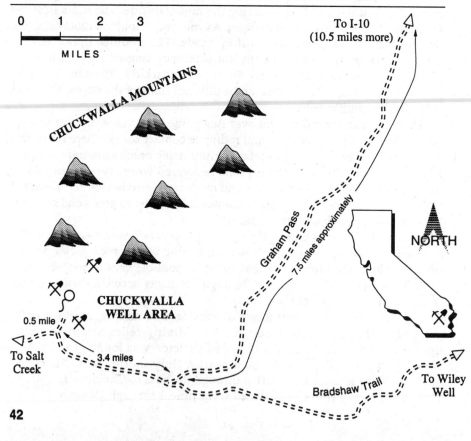

A rare desert oasis near the Chuckwalla/Mule Mountain area.

Rockhounding: Agate, in a variety of colors and patterns, may be found upon the hills and all along their bases. Jasper in orangish red, yellow, maroon, and green will be located here too.

The well is a gathering place for many desert animals, as well as one of the few places for them to drink. Try to park away from the well so as not to disturb their comings and goings. The best collecting is away from the well and along the hillsides behind it.

SITE 9 *PSILOMELANE AT ARLINGTON MINE*

Land type: Desert mountains.
Best season: Late September to May.
Tools: Rock pick, collecting bag.
Material: Botryoidal psilomelane.
Lore: New Age believers maintain that psilomelane, worn or carried, enhances psychic vision and development.
Special attraction: Giant Indian intaglios (desert drawings).
Elevation: 1,100 feet.
Land Manager: BLM.
Vehicle type: Any.
For more information: USGS maps Arlington Mine and Inca quadrangles; BLM's Parker/Blythe Desert Access Guide #16.
Finding the site: To get to the Arlington Mine, exit Interstate 10 at Lovekin Road and head north (as the road takes a northwesterly direction it becomes Midland Road). Drive Lovekin/Midland Road for 18 miles to a huge white boulder of gypsum to your left. Turn left here and head west. At 1.6 miles you will cross a railroad track and enter what remains of the small burg of Inca. Just past the tracks, another 0.1 mile, take the right fork and continue west for 9 miles on P172 (at one time a fully paved road).

Small piles of a white substance litter the road on both the left and right. This is gypsum from the U.S. Gypsum Mine, 3 miles to the north on a slope of the Little Maria Mountains. At your 9-mile mark you will take a road to your left heading to some diggings on the flank of a broad, low mountain. The road will lead straight to the diggings. You may park or continue on up to several higher levels. Psilomelane, one of the principle ores of manganese, litters the ground and is piled up everywhere.

Rockhounding: The Arlington Mine actually composes a group of several claims and diggings that were active during World Wars I and II. However, the first and largest site is usually referred to as the Arlington Mine. Manganese, a major component of psilomelane, is used to harden steel and in the manufacture of armaments. The mine is currently inactive. Look for velvety black botryoidal masses or semi-metallic pieces as specimens or cutting material.

If you cut across the botryoidal mass, shaping and polishing will result in a gemstone with the silvery look and luster of hematite, but displaying char-

SITE 9 *PSILOMELANE AT ARLINGTON MINE*

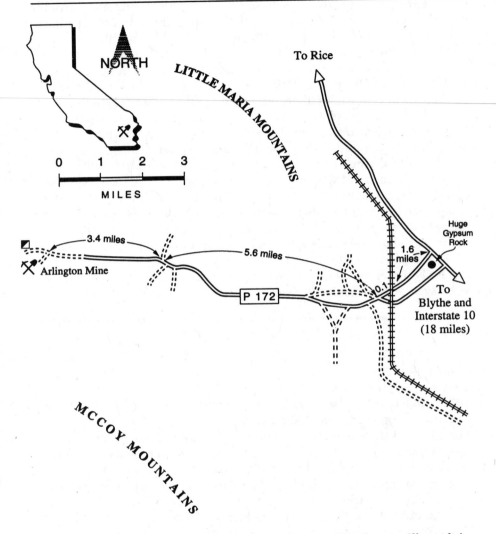

coal-colored, concentric rings. Working up the metallic pieces will result in a heavy gem comparable to silver-colored hematite. Psilomelane is slightly softer than hematite, 5 on the Mohs scale, but makes a beautiful and unique gem, as well as an interesting and unusual addition to a mineral collection.

Also at the Arlington Mine, thin mantles of drusy quartz and chalcedony form in layers within contact zones between the psilomelane and the country rock. These can be found littering the ground or attached to the psilomelane fragments. In the case of the Arlington Mine site, the best psilomelane collecting seemed to be on the lower levels in and around the parking area. Easy pickin's! Just drive to the site, step out, stoop over, and pick it up. What could be better?

There are psilomelane diggings farther out P172, which are visible on the flanks of the low mountains to the left of the road. Just previous to my visit to the mine, in early 1994, heavy rains and flash flooding had partially destroyed portions of P172 beyond the first site. Although I visited these other digs, a 4X4 was required. P172 is maintained by the BLM and may have been repaired since my visit.

Although much of the diggings comprising the Arlington Mine area appear to have been strip mined, there is the occasional tunnel and shaft, so be cautious in your explorations. Although I saw no other vehicles on P172 in early 1994, the road is used by large mining vehicles when the U.S. Gypsum Mine is active. Be ready to yield the right of way if necessary.

To get to the larger-than-life Giant Indian intaglios (pronounced in-TAL-ios) return to Blythe and take California 95 approximately 12 miles north of Blythe. To the right will be a large stone monument with a brass plaque describing the intaglios. To get to the intaglios turn left across the highway and proceed east on a well-graded dirt road for a short distance, until you see several fenced areas to the right. A short and easy walk will bring you to the fenced intaglios. The intaglios were traced into the desert pavement by ancient peoples and are protected by fencing from trespass. Their shapes are easily discerned from the ground and spectacular from the air, should you have the opportunity to fly over them.

SITE 10 *OROCOPIA BLOODSTONE*

Land type: Desert hills.
Best season: November to April.
Tools: Collecting bag, rock pick, crack hammer.
Material: Bloodstone, red and green jasper.
Lore: Legend states that green jasper was placed at the foot of the cross and was flecked with blood from Christ's wounds, thereby becoming bloodstone. Worn, bloodstone draws wealth, predicts weather, aids in legal battles, eases labor pains, increases crop yield, and stanches bleeding when held to a wound. Popular during biblical times, it was called heliotrope.
Special attraction: The historic Bradshaw Trail area.
Elevation: 1,400 feet.
Land manager: BLM.
Vehicle type: 4X4.
For more information: BLM's Desert Access Guide Chuckwalla #18; USGS map Hayfield Quadrangle.
Finding the site: From Interstate 10 exit at Red Cloud Road. Drive 13.8 miles along the Mining Railroad. Part of the drive will be through a wide, sandy wash. Turn right into a canyon and drive a few hundred yards to a BLM sign that tells you not to drive any farther. From here you will walk a couple hundred yards to the northwest to where two washes converge. On the slope between the two washes you will find abundant bloodstone.

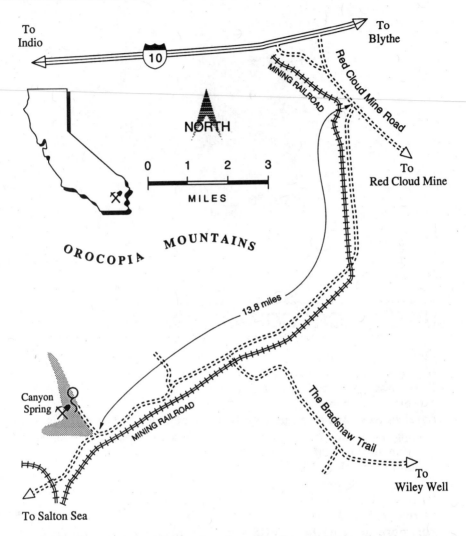

Rockhounding: The site is abundant in red and green jasper in many patterns, much with red jasper flecks. Also found is green jasper with translucent white agate and dark green jasper with bold jagged lines, much like lightening bolts.

This area is completely closed from June 1 to November 1, so plan your visit from November 2 through May 31, although November through April are more comfortably cool.

This area has a small spring that seeps all year long, making it an essential watering place for desert wildlife when other springs in the area dry up during the hot summer season.

Orocopia bloodstone. Rough and polished cabochon.

SITE 11 *OROCOPIA FLUORSPAR*

Land type: Desert hills.
Best season: October to April.
Tools: Rock pick, collecting bag.
Material: Fluorspar.
Lore: In New Age lore fluorite assists mental function and allays mental fatigue. It is useful to keep near computers, as it is reputed to enhance their function and prevent breakdowns.
Special attraction: None.
Elevation: 2,400 feet.
Land manager: BLM.
Vehicle type: 4X4.
For more information: USGS map Orocopia Canyon Quadrangle.
Finding the site: From Chiriaco Summit, exit, and just south of the freeway, take the road heading west 1.3 miles to a dirt road. Take this dirt road (SR2013) south 1.8 miles. It will branch left. Take this left branch southeast 1.4 miles. Again it will branch left. Take this left branch 1.8 miles. Turn right off of SR2013 onto a poorly-maintained and rocky road heading up the hill. Drive 0.2 miles or, if you can, a bit farther, until the road heads sharply uphill. Park at the base of this incline. On foot follow a narrow wash that is about 3 feet deep and lies to the right of the road. Walk this wash about 50 feet, then hike a short way up to the top of the hill on your right. Here you will find a shallow pit with vast quantities of fluorspar.

SITE 11 OROCOPIA FLUORSPAR

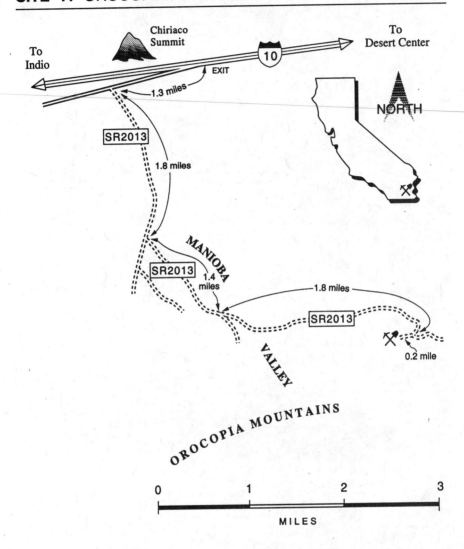

Rockhounding: This is the site of a long-abandoned fluorspar mine. Fluorspar, a variety of fluorite that crystallizes in needle-like crystals rather than the more common cubic variety, is used in steel and ceramic making.

Today fluorite is used in jewelry. Although a little on the soft side, it does make lovely jewelry and cabochons. The fluorspar from this site, when sawed into slabs, is suitable for lapidary projects. It is translucent to clear in cream, yellow, green, brown, and violet. My favorite is the cream with violet banding. The material from this location also makes nice tumbled pieces for the kids' jewelry projects. It will fluoresce under an ultraviolet lamp.

Author at Orocopia fluorspar site.

Author's Note: This site is now closed.

SITE 13 *BIG RIVER BOTRYOIDAL CHALCEDONY WITH DRUSY QUARTZ, JASPER, AND AGATE*

Land type: Desert.
Best season: October through April.
Tools: Rock bag, pick.
Material: Botryoidal chalcedony with drusy quartz, jasper, and agate.
Lore: Chalcedony and drusy quarts offer protection during travel and freedom from nightmares. Jasper is the rain bringer and healer of bodily ills.
Special attractions: Colorado River camping and recreation.
Elevation: 1,180 feet.
Land manager: BLM.
Vehicle type: Any.
For more information: BLM's Parker/Blythe Access Guide #16; USGS maps Parker and Parker NW quadrangles.
Finding the site: From California 62, as you're heading east, proceed 2.3 miles past Rio Mesa Road and turn left (north) onto a dirt road with a sign reading "Private Access Road." This road is maintained by the water district and goes to the Colorado River Aqueduct. You are permitted to travel on this road to get to the collecting site. Drive north for 4 miles and turn right just past the bee hives, heading 0.2 miles to the base of a hill. The area west of the hill has been graded. Nice specimens of botryoidal chalcedony in both cream and pink, with a sparkling coating of drusy quartz crystals, will be found in varying sizes.

SITE 13 *BIG RIVER BOTRYOIDAL CHALCEDONY WITH DRUSY QUARTZ, JASPER, AND AGATE*

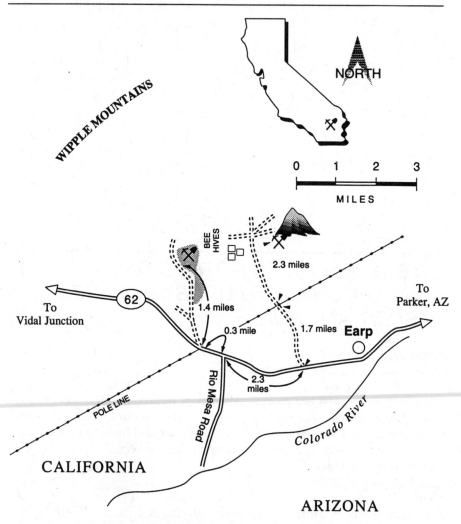

To reach another nearby collecting location with jasper and agate, head 0.3 miles west past Rio Mesa Road. Turn right and head north for 1.4 miles. (Ignore the road heading in a westerly direction at 0.6 miles.) This site yields red jasper and a variety of pink and white agate.

Rockhounding: The first site at 2.3 miles east of Rio Mesa Road is reputed to have excellent red, yellow, and rainbow jasper among an abundance of very poor, grainy material. Perhaps this was true many years ago. On my visit in the spring of 1994, although I searched the area, I found only very poor quality jasper. The area may be more productive after a heavy rain just

Beavertail cactus in bloom near Big River site.

north of the foot of the mountain. At present there is a chain across the opening of the wash, so you will not be able to drive into it. The only item of interest in this area is the sparkling, drusy-quartz-covered chalcedony in both pink and cream. This material will make nice baroque pins, pendants, and bolas if the edges are ground and smoothed and a silver or gold bezel is added.

The second location, 0.3 miles west of Rio Mesa Road, is the more productive of the two as far as agate and jasper are concerned. To the east of the road about 50 feet is a shallow wash. I had my best luck collecting along the length of this wash. Here is found mottled pink and cream, as well as red and cream, agate along with a few pieces of red jasper. Also there were some scattered pieces of white chalcedony with gray banding. Some walking and looking is required as the material is not abundant. After 20 minutes of walking about you may find a nice collection of cutting material. This is not a trip to take in and of itself. However, if you are vacationing in the Colorado River area, this trip makes a nice break from nearby water recreation.

If you are planning a trip to this area during the first two weeks of April, bring your camera and photograph the beautiful and vibrantly pink and fuchsia blooms on the beavertail cacti that line the road leading to the more productive of the two locations.

SITE 14 *TURTLE MOUNTAINS SNOWY CHALCEDONY ROSES*

Land type: Desert.
Best season: October to April.
Tools: Rock pick, collecting bag.
Material: Snowy-white desert roses.
Lore: Purity and good dreams.
Special attraction: Turtle Mountains.
Elevation: 1,312 feet.
Land manager: BLM.
Vehicle type: Any.
For more information: BLM's Desert Access guides Blythe/Parker #16 and Needles #13; USGS maps Stepladder Mountains and Snaggletooth quadrangles.
Finding the site: From U.S. Highway 95 turn west onto Turtle Mountain Road. Head west along the well-maintained dirt road. Anywhere between 9 and 10.5 miles snowy white chalcedony roses are found along the side of the road.

Rockhounding: This site is located near the spectacular Turtle Mountains. The material found here is snowy white chalcedony, much of which forms into the delightful rose shapes sought by collectors and lapidaries. The white

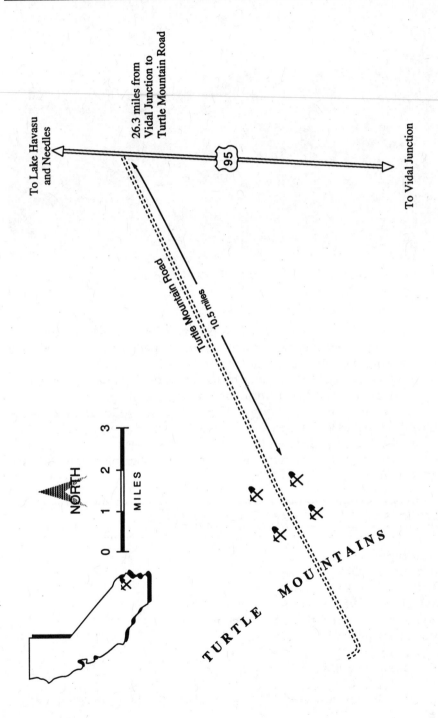

The interesting geography and vistas of the Turtle Mountains.

roses, with just a little smoothing of the edges, make lovely settings for black pearls or any colorful spherical or baroque-shaped gemstone. Roses are naturals for bolas, pins, and pendants.

A scattering of agate and jasper can also be found, but as a rule are scarce along the road. I found a beautiful piece of moss agate.

Any vehicle can make the drive on Turtle Mountain Road. There are some sandy spots, but as long as you keep moving you will have no trouble. Should you decide to explore some of the washes you will need a 4X4. Bring your camera, as the Turtle Mountains make excellent photographic subjects in the changing light.

SITE 15 *LAKE HAVASU AGATE*

Land type: Desert.
Best season: October to April.
Tools: Rock pick, collecting bag.
Material: Colorful agate.
Lore: Courage, strength, and protection.
Special attraction: Lake Havasu.
Elevation: 918 feet.
Land manager: BLM.
Vehicle type: 4X4.
For more information: BLM's Desert Access Guide Parker/Blythe #16.

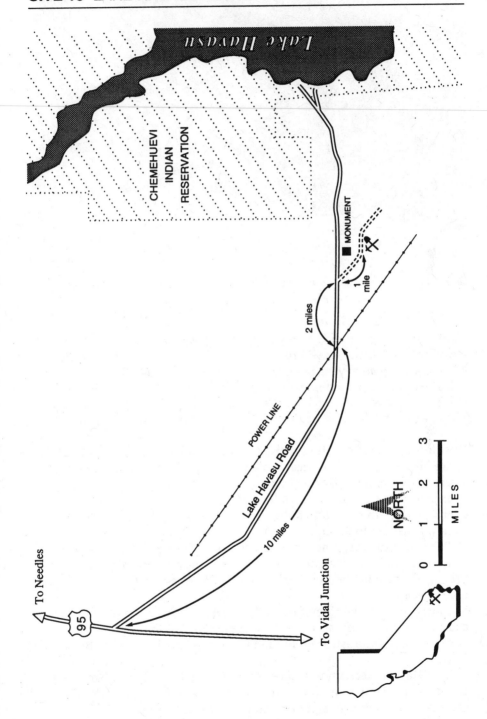

Colorful agates fill ravine (center of photo).

Finding the site: From U.S. Highway 95 turn east onto Lake Havasu Road. Drive east for 10 miles to where the powerlines cross the road. Drive 2 more miles to a dirt road to your right. Shortly after you turn onto this dirt road you will see a large rock monument which reads "Havasu Mining and Minerals." Drive 1 mile to the hill which will be marked with streaks of light-colored ash. The entire hill is made of agate and jasper in many patterns and colors.

Rockhounding: This site is a great place to collect agate and jasper. The entire hill rising from the wash is composed of colorful agate and jasper in a variety of hues and patterns. The road is firm, and any vehicle can make it, except for the last 0.2 to 0.3 miles. The agate and jasper hill is located in a large wash, which will make a 4X4 necessary unless you are willing to walk the last 0.2 to 0.3 miles.

The collecting material comes in fist to boulder sizes. There is plenty to pick up. The highly energetic may wish to bring chisels, sledges, and gads to remove agate insitu, but there is so much just laying about that it is not really necessary.

Somewhere on the side of the hill near the second seam of white ash is a small deposit of chrysocolla. I was unable to find the deposit. However, near the base of the ash seam I found numerous small pieces of chrysocolla float.

Lake Havasu Recreation Area is on the Chemehuevi Indian Reservation. To visit the lake or camp there, you will need to obtain a permit. Permits can be obtained at a gate prior to entering the recreation area.

SITE 16 *DENDRITIC WHITE OPALITE AT GOFFS*

Land type: Desert hills.
Best season: October to April.
Tools: Rock pick, collecting bag.
Material: Dendritic white opalite, agate, jasper.
Lore: Balances left and right brain hemispheres and lightly stimulates the glands.
Special attraction: None.
Elevation: 3,200 feet.
Land manager: BLM.
Vehicle type: Any.
For more information: BLM's Desert Access Guide New York Mountains #9; USGS map Goffs Quadrangle.
Finding the site: You may access Goffs Road from either Interstate 40 or U.S. Highway 95. From Goffs road, near the tiny town of Goffs, turn onto Lanfair Road and head north 11 miles. Park along the road where the wash crosses it. Slightly farther on you will cross a cattle guard and come to a second, less productive wash.

Rockhounding: This site is located in free-range cattle country, so exercise caution when driving on Lanfair Road. When you exit your car at the collecting site, you may see cattle about. Not being familiar with bovine protocol, I adopted the policy of ignoring them. It must have been the right thing to do, because they ignored me as well. Mind you, these happened to be all cows with calves. The ignoring policy may not work with bulls, so use caution when collecting near cattle.

Nice palm-sized pieces of white opalite with black dendrites are found in the wash, particularly on the east side of the road where the wash enters a rocky canyon. (The cows also favor this side of the wash). White opalite with translucent, amber-colored agate centers can occasionally be found also, plus some red jasper.

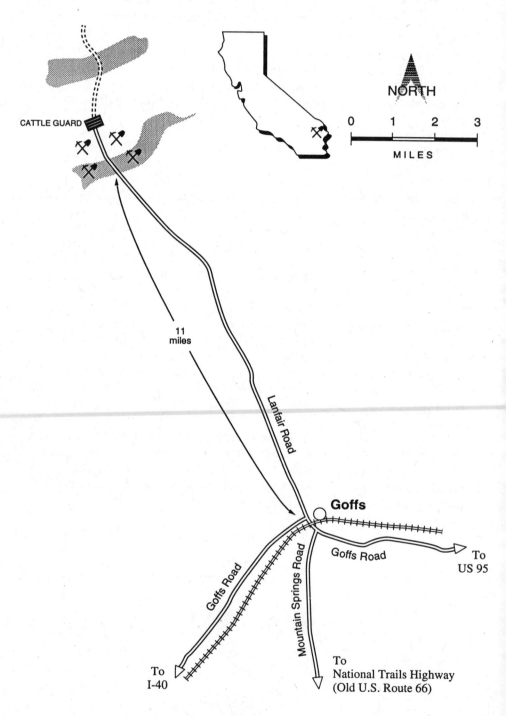

CATTLE GUARD

NORTH

0   1   2   3
MILES

11 miles

Lanfair Road

Goffs

Goffs Road

To
US 95

Goffs Road

Mountain Springs Road

To
National Trails Highway
(Old U.S. Route 66)

To
I-40

SITE 17 *DANBY OPALITE AND AGATE*

Land type: Desert hills.
Best season: October to April.
Tools: Collecting bag, rock pick, shovel.
Material: Colorful opalite and agate.
Lore: Opalite is mildly stimulating to the glandular system. Agate encourages strength, courage, and protection.
Special attraction: None.
Elevation: 1,300 feet.
Land manager: BLM.
Vehicle type: Any.
For more information: BLM's Desert Access Guide Sheephole Mountains #12; USGS maps Danby, Skeleton Pass, and Cadiz Summit quadrangles.
Finding the site: From National Trails Highway (formerly U.S. Highway 66) take Danby Road southeast for 1.7 miles. After crossing the railroad tracks, turn right, taking the road that runs parallel to the railroad tracks for 6.8 miles. Turn left onto a dirt road and travel 0.5 miles. I have marked this road with two rock cairns on the left. This dirt road is traversable by any vehicle. The other dirt roads in the area require a 4X4.

Double cairn erected by author at turnoff to the Danby opalite and agate site.

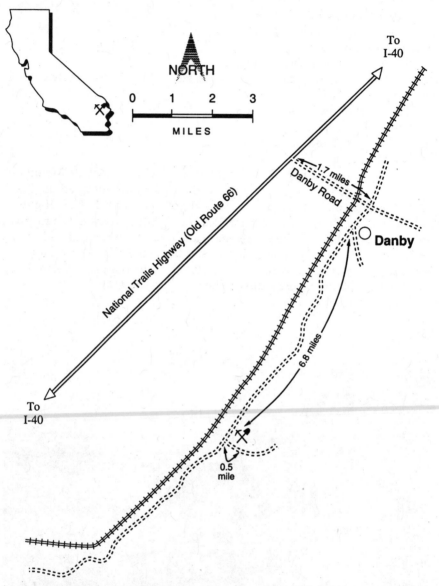

Rockhounding: The opalite and agate are most abundant on the left side of the road at 0.5 miles. Plenty of small sizes, ready for the tumbler, are found here. There are some larger pieces found above ground as well. Use your shovel to dig into the soft, fine sand for larger pieces.

The material comes in a variety of colors and patterns. The agate here is particularly beautiful in translucent red and orange shades. Most of the opalite occurs in rose pink and white.

SITE 18 *FOSSIL TRILOBITES AND MARBLE AT CADIZ*

Land type: Desert hills.
Best season: October to April.
Tools: Rock pick, collecting bag, chisel.
Material: Fossil trilobites, fossil algae, red marble.
Lore: Fossils, also called "draconites" and "witch stones," were believed to enhance longevity.
Special attraction: None.
Elevation: 918 feet.
Land manager: BLM.
Vehicle type: Any, 4X4.
For more information: BLM's Desert Access guides Providence Mountains #12 and Sheephole Mountains #15; USGS map Cadiz Summit Quadrangle.
Finding the site: From National Trails Highway (formerly U.S. Highway 66) turn southeast onto Cadiz Road. Drive the paved road for 4.3 miles. To get to the fossil site, turn left onto a dirt road heading in a northerly direction for 0.7 miles. (Ignore the road on the right at 0.4 miles.) At 0.7 miles turn onto the dirt road to your right. At 0.2 miles stay left and continue another 0.8 miles. You will see black buttes ahead. The fossils are located by

Comparing fossil finds at Cadiz fossil trilobite beds.

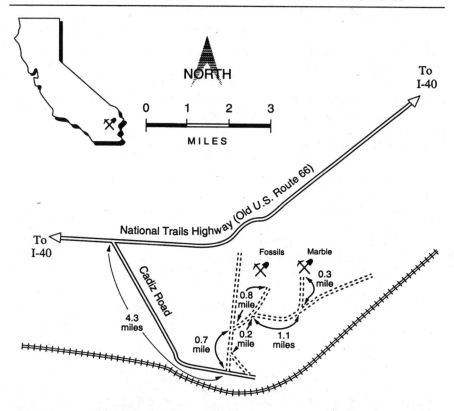

walking up the road to several shale deposits. The thick shale pieces can be "opened" to reveal trilobite casts and molds by turning the shale on end and gently tapping the edge. The shale will split revealing a trilobite form.

A 4X4 will be needed to get to the marble site, as you will have to drive a sandy wash. Return to 0.2 miles where a dirt road took off to the right in a northeasterly direction. Drive this road for 1.1 miles and turn left at the rock cairn and drive up out of the wash, following the road to the small marble quarry ahead.

Rockhounding: The fossil trilobite site has long been a favorite of rockhounds, with an abundant supply of casts and molds of these ancient sea creatures. Recently, however, the fossil shales have been mined and most have been removed. It is still possible to find fossil trilobites by sifting through the broken shale left by the miners. Fossil algae is found in this area as well. Look for a gray stone with black whorls. This is the fossil algae.

The red marble site yields a moderate grade marble in a deep burgundy red or white with red flecks. You will need a 4X4 to get to this site, as access is through a sandy wash.

SITE 19 *MARBLE MOUNTAINS GARNET AND HEMATITE*

Land type: Desert hills.
Best season: October to May.
Tools: Rock pick, chisel, collecting bag.
Material: Garnet, hematite, epidote.
Lore: Garnet was believed to enhance strength and healing by way of enhancing the blood. Hematite is the bloodstone referred to in the Bible because of its red streak when drawn across tile. Epidote, like jade, was used to attract wealth.
Special attraction: None.
Elevation: 1,200 feet.
Land manager: BLM.
Vehicle type: Sturdy truck or 4X4.
For more information: USGS map Cadiz Quadrangle.
Finding the site: From National Trails Highway (Old Route 66) head 0.3 miles west of the Cadiz turnoff. Turn north (right) and drive 0.5 miles. Turn right and drive 0.3 miles. Turn left and drive 2.3 miles north, ignoring all other roads to the right or left. A small, brown mountain contains seams of garnets, particularly in the open pockets.

Garnets loose and in matrix from Garnet Hill site near Chamblis.

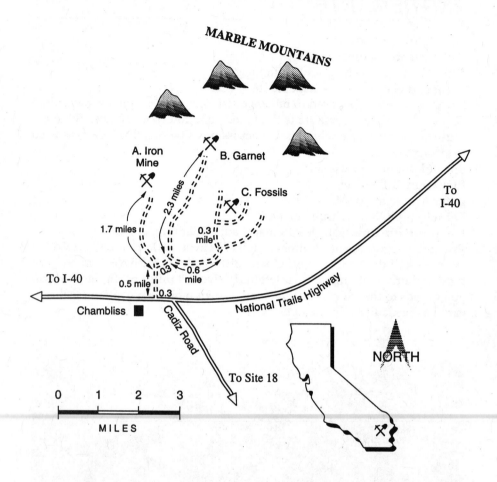

Rockhounding: This site offers small to large garnets of pink, red, and brown. The small garnets are suitable for faceting, while the large ones, left in matrix, make great display pieces. The large garnets are too fractured and opaque to make nice faceted gems. Use your chisel to remove the garnet containing matrix. Also sift through the dirt at the bottom of the pockets for loose garnets.

The green, platy stone scattered about is epidote. It has no jewelry value in and of itself. It is, however, one of the eight earth-forming minerals and, because of this, makes a nice addition to a serious mineral collection.

Much of the epidote contains blades of metallic hematite, also desirable for mineral collectors. Larger chunks of hematite are found in the area, and these are suitable for lapidary uses.

SITE 20 KELBAKER ROAD NODULES AND CHALCEDONY

Land type: Desert hills.
Best season: October to April.
Tools: Rock pick, collecting bag, shovel.
Material: Nodules, chalcedony.
Lore: Chalcedony was believed to protect travelers and to prevent nightmares. Nodules, like geodes, might have been thought to be the abodes of elemental spirits and female energy due to their egg-like shapes.
Special attraction: None.
Elevation: 2,600 feet.
Land manager: BLM.
Vehicle type: 4X4.
For more information: USGS maps Brown Buttes and Amboy quadrangles.
Finding the site: To get to Site A from National Trails Highway, head north on Kelbaker Road. At 1.6 miles turn east (right) and drive 0.1 miles. Turn north (left) and drive 0.9 miles. Turn east (right) and drive 1 mile. To reach the other collecting areas at Site A merely return 1 mile to the north-heading road and take other faintly marked roads going east. Chalcedony roses are scattered about the desert pavement. The concentrations are not great, but a little easy walking will net you some nice ones.

To get to Site B drive an additional 5.7 miles north from Site A on Kelbaker Road. Take a road that heads northeast for 1.6 miles. Nodules and some geodes may be found by digging into the hillside. Some of these geodes are reported to have crystal centers. I, however, didn't find any of those on my trip in May of 1994. Chalcedony is scattered around the areas at the base of the hill.

Rockhounding: Rockhounds visited this site extensively in the past. However, in recent years there haven't been many trips to this area. The scarcity of activity, as well as erosion by wind and rain, has allowed the area to accumulate some more material for rockhounds to collect.

The aforementioned processes of erosion have not improved the road to Site B. It is recommended that you use a 4X4 to reach this site.

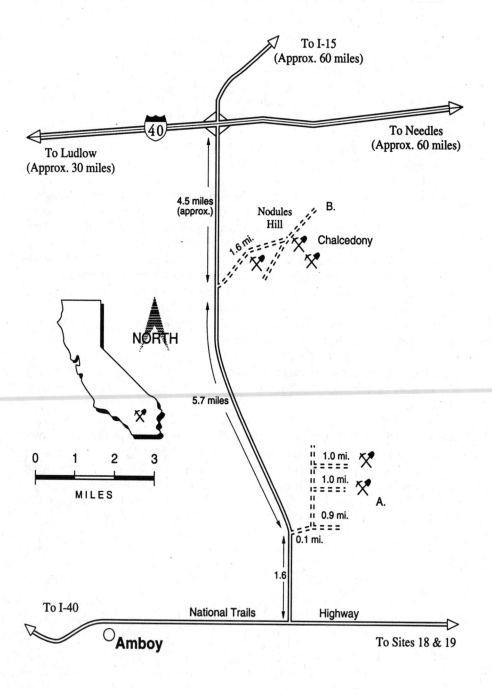

To I-15
(Approx. 60 miles)

40

To Needles
(Approx. 60 miles)

To Ludlow
(Approx. 30 miles)

4.5 miles
(approx.)

Nodules
Hill

B.

1.6 mi.

Chalcedony

NORTH

5.7 miles

0   1   2   3

MILES

1.0 mi.

1.0 mi.

A.

0.9 mi.

0.1 mi.

1.6

To I-40

National Trails

Highway

Amboy

To Sites 18 & 19

SITE 21 *PROVIDENCE MOUNTAINS IRON MINERALS*

Land type: Desert Hills.
Best season: October to April.
Tools: Rock pick, collecting bag, chisel, crack hammer.
Material: Pyrite, hematite, galena.
Lore: Hematite was thought to cure anemia, while pyrite was worn or carried to bring luck and wealth. Galena, an ore of lead, was believed to ease nervous disorders.
Special attraction: Mitchell Caverns.
Elevation: 2,600 feet.
Land manager: BLM.
Vehicle type: 4X4.
For more information: USGS maps Fountain Peak and Colton Well quadrangles.
Finding the site: To get to the Vulcan Mine, exit at Kelbaker Road from Interstate 40 and head north for approximately 18 miles. Be sure to bear right in order to remain on Kelbaker Road. Turn sharp right onto Vulcan Mine Road and drive 5 miles.

To get to the Bonanza King Mine, exit Interstate 40 at the Essex offramp and head northwest 10.8 miles on Essex Road. Turn right and take this road 4.7 miles. Ignore the road to the right and continue an additional 1.9 miles to the dumps.

Rockhounding: At the Vulcan Mine dumps, iron ores may be collected. Pyrite and hematite are of interest to lapidaries as well as collectors. You will need your chisel and crack hammer, in some cases, to remove specimens from seams in boulders. Mineral collectors may also be interested in the other colorful red and yellow mining by-products, such as limonite and magnetite. Epidote is the green material and may be of interest to collectors also, as it is one of the eight earth-building minerals.

The Bonanza King Mine dumps also have pyrite and the lead ore, galena. While in this area, you must see the nearby Mitchell Caverns. Guided tours are available. DO NOT collect any fossils while within the Mitchell Caverns area.

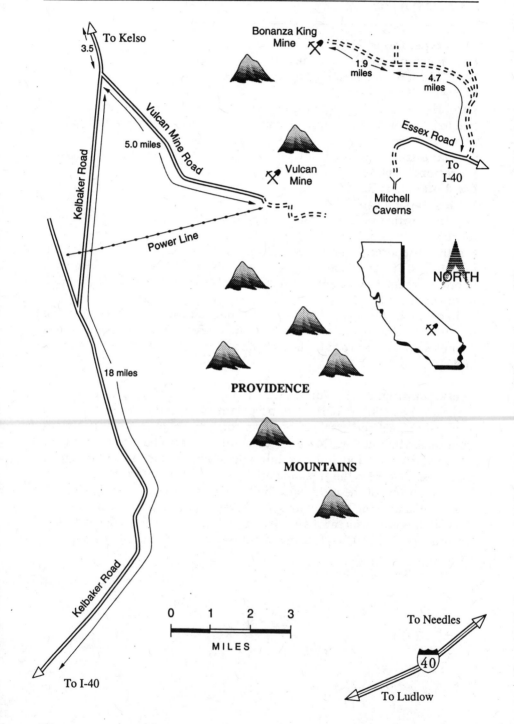

To Kelso

3.5

Bonanza King
Mine

1.9 miles

4.7 miles

Vulcan Mine Road

5.0 miles

Kelbaker Road

Vulcan Mine

Essex Road

To I-40

Mitchell Caverns

Power Line

NORTH

18 miles

PROVIDENCE

MOUNTAINS

Kelbaker Road

0   1   2   3

MILES

To Needles

40

To I-40

To Ludlow

SITE 22 *OLD CAMP CARNELIAN AND CHALCEDONY ROSES*

Land type: Desert.
Best season: October to April.
Tools: Rock pick, collecting bag.
Material: Carnelian, chalcedony roses.
Lore: Carnelian brought protection and peace, while chalcedony roses would likely have the same attributes as plain chalcedony by protecting from nightmares and also as a protection to travelers.
Special attraction: None.
Elevation: 1,450 feet.
Land manager: BLM.
Vehicle type: 4X4.
For more information: USGS map Ash Hill Quadrangle.
Finding the site: From Ludlow drive 9.2 miles in an easterly direction on National Trails Highway (Old Route 66). Turn right and drive 0.6 miles.

Rockhounding: Here you will find carnelian, a type of agate, in translucent to opaque cream, yellow, orange, and orangish red. The road has not been maintained for some time and was very washed out during my 1994 spring visit. Near the collecting area, you will see remains of an old camp.

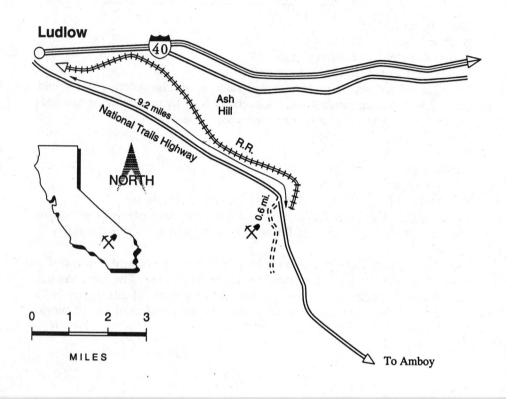

Ludlow

40

9.2 miles

National Trails Highway

Ash
Hill

R.R.

NORTH

0.6 mi.

To Amboy

0   1   2   3

MILES

SITE 23 *LUDLOW GEMS*

Land type: Desert.
Best season: October to May.
Tools: Rock pick, collecting bag.
Material: Jasper, agate, manganese, calcite, copper minerals.
Lore: Jasper and agate bring courage and strength. Manganese ores are believed, in New Age philosophies, to enhance psychic development. Calcite was thought to assist in purifying the body during fasting. Copper and its minerals were used to enhance healing and the growth of plants.
Special attraction: None.
Elevation: 1,980 feet.
Land manager: BLM.
Vehicle type: 4X4.
For more information: USGS maps Broadwell Dry Lake and Ludlow quadrangles.
Finding the site: From Ludlow head north on Crucero Road 0.9 miles. Turn left and head west 1 mile. Here you will find jasper along the base of the hills. Back out on Crucero Road, head 1.3 miles farther, turn left again and drive west 1.3 miles. At this location you will find manganese minerals and some calcite in seams. Here, too, is some jasper. This comprises Site E.

To get to sites A and B return to Crucero Road and head north for another 3.7 miles. Take the road that branches to the left 1.9 miles, then turn left and continue 3.2 miles. At the fork, go left 1.4 miles to find agate.

To get to Site C return to the fork at 1.4 miles and this time go right. Drive 2 miles on the right fork, and here you will find more agate and some jasper.

To find Site D return to the road that branched off of Crucero Road. Drive north another 1.7 miles and turn west (left). Drive 0.6 miles, turning right. For more copper minerals, return to the 0.6 mile point again to the west heading road. You may drive another 0.6 miles farther west, turning right and going 0.2 miles north for more copper minerals.

Rockhounding: These sites offer a variety of colorful agate, as well a moss and lace varieties. Red jasper, chalcedony, and colorful common opal may also be found at these sites.

Here, too, you will find manganese minerals and calcite, which fluoresce under ultraviolet light. The copper minerals that may be found include bornite, malachite, cuprite, and chrysocolla. There is also some more calcite and some hematite at the copper minerals location.

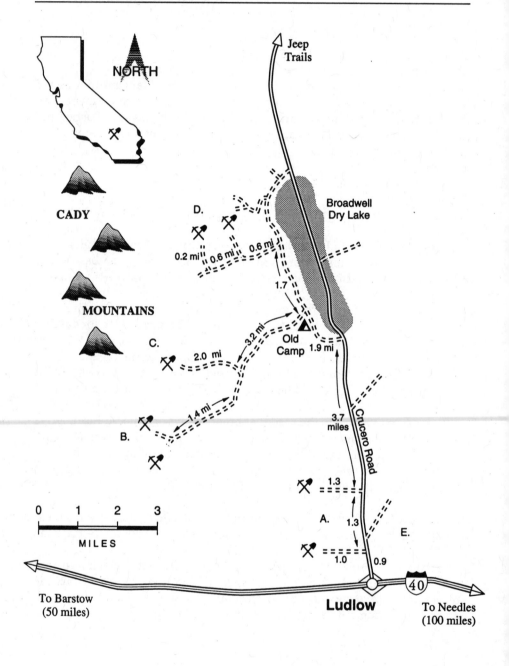

NORTH

CADY

MOUNTAINS

Jeep Trails

Broadwell Dry Lake

D.

0.2 mi   0.6 mi   0.6 mi

1.7

3.2 mi

Old Camp   1.9 mi

C.   2.0 mi

1.4 mi

B.

3.7 miles

Crucero Road

1.3

A.   1.3

E.

1.0   0.9

0   1   2   3

MILES

To Barstow (50 miles)

Ludlow

40

To Needles (100 miles)

SITE 24 *WEST OF LUDLOW CHALCEDONY, CALCITE, AND MORE*

Land type: Desert.
Best season: October to April.
Tools: Rock pick, collecting bag.
Material: Colorful jasper, agate, chalcedony, calcite.
Lore: Jasper, agate, and chalcedony all have protective qualities. Calcite was worn to assist the purification of the body during fasting.
Special attraction: None.
Elevation: 1,900 feet.
Land manager: BLM.
Vehicle type: 4X4.
For more information: USGS maps Ludlow and Broadwell Dry Lake quadrangles.
Finding the site: You can access this site by driving west of Ludlow on National Trails Highway (Old Route 66) 3.6 miles. This will put you at the first turnoff to one of many sites with plentiful collecting material. Head north and follow the mileages given on the accompanying map to reach the varied collecting areas.

To reach additional sites, you may continue on National Trails Highway an additional 1.5 miles and head north, following the mileages on the map to even more collecting sites.

Rockhounding: This site, with its varied collecting spots and colorful material, has long been a favorite of rockhounds. The material is still plentiful in most places. The agate and jasper are colorful, in reds, yellows, greens, and oranges, with black and brown banding.

Check boulder seams, in all locations, for calcite crystallizing in the rhombohedral form.

This area is reputed to have rainbow jasper and Iceland spar. Even though I did not find any, you might. I did not linger long enough in the area to do it full justice. A day is just not enough to fully cover the area. Plan to spend several days, if you can.

SITE 24 *WEST OF LUDLOW CHALCEDONY, CALCITE, AND MORE*

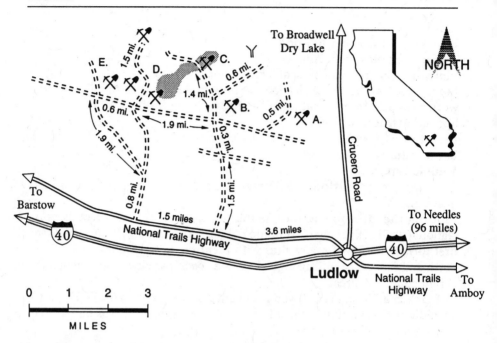

SITE 25 *HECTOR AGATES AND JASPER*

Land type: Desert hills.
Best season: October to April.
Tools: Rock pick, collecting bag, rake.
Material: Agate, jasper.
Lore: Agate and jasper brought courage, strength, and protection. Jasper was used by Native Americans to bring rain.
Special attraction: Pisgah Crater volcanic tube exploration.
Elevation: 2,004 feet.
Land manager: BLM.
Vehicle type: 4X4.
For more information: USGS maps Hector and Sunshine Peak quadrangles.

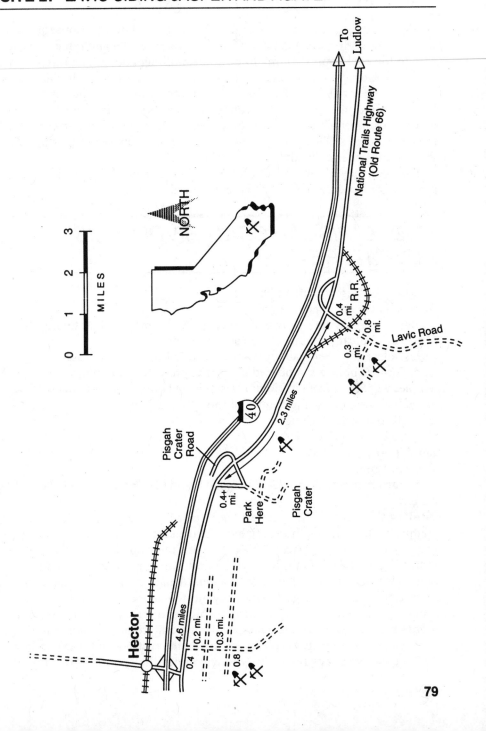

Finding the site: On National Trails Highway (Old Route 66), drive 0.4 miles east of the Hector turnoff. Turn off National Trails Highway south (right) and drive 0.2 miles, ignoring the gas line road which crosses the road you are on. Drive an additional 0.3 miles and turn west (right). Drive 0.8 miles. Do not drive off of the road; it is very sandy.

Rockhounding: This site is an old favorite of rockhounds. Consequently, much material has been gathered over the years. Still some remains available to the rockhound willing to do some walking about. The farther you walk, the more you will collect. Bring your lunch, spend the day, and plan to get some exercise. A rake will enable you to gather those pieces that are lying unseen, just beneath the sandy surface. If you plan your trip after desert storms, your search will be easier because more material will be freshly exposed. This is a good area to visit as part of a week-long trip, while visiting the other collecting sites in this area.

Here you may collect, in addition to the agate, jasper, but also occasional pieces of chalcedony and some common opal.

SITE 26 *PISGAH CRATER VOLCANIC ADVENTURE*

Land type: Desert plateau basalts.
Best season: October to April.
Tools: Rock pick, collecting bag, flashlights, gloves, hard hat, hiking shoes.
Material: Volcanic bombs, lava rock, goethite.
Lore: Volcanic rocks of all types are associated with the Hawaiian goddess, Pele. Because of lava's supposed powers of protection and magic, altars and temples were built from it. Holding a stone containing goethite was supposed to enable one to hear the "music of the spheres."
Special attraction: None.
Elevation: 2,100 feet.
Land manager: BLM.
Vehicle type: Any.
For more information: USGS maps Sunshine Peak and Lavic Lake quadrangles.
Finding the site: Exit Interstate 40 at Hector Road and onto National Trails Highway. On National Trails Highway drive east 4.6 miles until you come to a paved road to your right. This is Pisgah Crater Road. You will see a sign indicating Twin Mountain Rock Company. Turn right and proceed for 0.4 plus miles. Here you will encounter a closed gate. Park your vehicle on the road to the right of the gate. Walk beyond the gate and along the road for a short distance. Look for a footpath heading east from the road. Follow this footpath as it heads around Pizgah volcanic crater and through a massive lava field, or basalt plateau. When you are on the east side of the crater, begin walking over the lava field. You will encounter the openings to many vol-

Geology student emerges from her volcanic tube adventure.

canic tubes. The walk to the tubes is approximately 0.75 miles from the paved road.

Rockhounding: Pisgah Crater has been the site of commercial mining activity for many years. The volcanic rock is used for the manufacture of paving material and for use in electric and gas barbecues, as briquettes.

You may look down into the bowl of the crater, from its east side at the lava tube field, but the most interesting feature is the lava field itself. Here you can collect volcanic bombs that were ejected thousands of years ago during the long-ago eruptions. Look for football-shaped rocks of varying sizes. Some of the lava rock is coated with metallic goethite in colors of gold, blue, and violet. Most of this goethite coating seems to be found near the parking area.

The volcanic lava tubes beckon to the adventurous. These are located on the eastern-most side of Pisgah. There are a variety of openings. Some are easier than others to enter. There are tubes to match most adventure levels.

The tubes are a labyrinth of interesting tunnels and rooms. Within the tubes is a register you may wish to sign and date, to mark the fact that you were there.

Wearing gloves while climbing in the tubes will protect your hands. A hard hat is recommended but not essential. Take a couple flashlights, extra batteries and bulbs, and a canteen of water. Above all be careful.

The walk from the paved road to the tubes is about three-quarters of a mile. Some of the trek will take you through deep sand and over low, steep hills. Good hiking boots are recommended.

This is a good spot to see "pahoehoe-" (pronounced pa-hoy-hoy) type lava flow. The Hawaiian people are familiar with volcanic eruptions and have words for describing the various types of lava. Geologists and volcanologists have adopted these descriptive words. Pahoehoe describes a thick, viscous lava that shows flow marks, ripples, and ropey coils. This is what you will see at Pisgah. The other type is "aa" (pronounced ah-ah). Aa describes a less viscous type, that cools into blocks, columns, or jagged cinders.

If you take this trip on a weekend, you will likely see groups of students camped along the road below the gate, as well as a bus or two parked near the gate. Pisgah is the pilgrimage site to which geology teachers from all over the state bring their students to study the mechanics of volcanism and explore the tubes. This is how I took my first volcanic-tube adventure, while studying geology at Chaffee College with Rod Parcel. I reprised this trip with partners Mo and Ed Hemler in the winter of 1994.

The parking area, near the gate, is also a great place to collect replacement briquettes for your barbecue.

SITE 27 *LAVIC SIDING JASPER AND AGATE*

Land type: Desert.
Best season: October to April.
Tools: Rock pick, collecting bag.
Material: Colorful jasper and agate.
Lore: Jasper and agate were carried by warriors to whom strength and courage were essential.
Special attraction: Pisgah Crater volcanic tube exploration.
Elevation: 1,900 feet.
Land manager: BLM.
Vehicle type: 4X4.
For more information: USGS maps Sunshine Peak and Lavic Lake quadrangles. See map on p. 79.
Finding the site: From National Trails Highway or Interstate 40 exit at Lavic Road and head south 0.4 miles. Cross the tracks and drive farther south 0.8 miles. Take the road to the west (right) for 0.3 miles.

Rockhounding: While this site is an old rockhound favorite, good material still remains. Here you can collect colorful jasper and agate in reds, blues, vibrant yellows, and oranges. Some of this material has showy white banding. Walk out into the desert, especially toward the west, and you many find more and larger pieces.

SITE 28 *WEST OF HECTOR BLUE CHALCEDONY, JASPER, AND AGATE*

Land type: Desert.
Best season: October to April.
Tools: Rock pick, collecting bag.
Material: Blue chalcedony, colorful agate, and jasper.
Lore: Blue chalcedony promotes sleep, healing, and calming of emotions. Agate and jasper were the stones of warriors and rain-makers.
Special attraction: Pisgah Crater volcanic tube exploration.
Elevation: 1,900 feet.
Land manager: BLM.
Vehicle type: 4X4.
For more information: USGS map Hector Quadrangle.
Finding the site: From National Trails Highway, or Interstate 40, take Hector Road north approximately 1 mile. Turn west (left) along the road paralleling the railroad tracks. Take this road west for 2 miles. The material lies north of the tracks and mostly up on a hill, which is about 0.5 miles north of the railroad tracks. You may park just south of the tracks and walk across them toward the orange-looking hill.

Rockhounding: Jasper will be found in warm shades of orange and yellow with banding in a variety of colors, including red. Chalcedony will be found in blue, as well as many other colors. However, this site is prized for the blue variety.

As always, use caution should you choose to drive your vehicle across the tracks.

SITE 28 *WEST OF HECTOR BLUE CHALCEDONY, JASPER, AND AGATE*

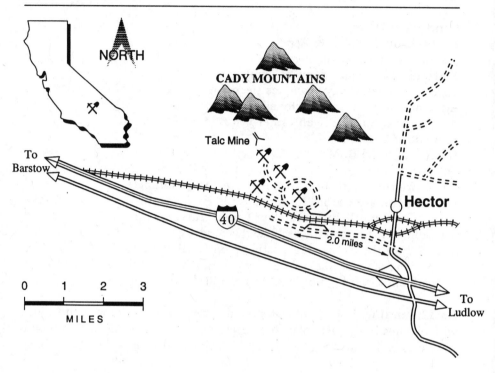

SITE 29 *NEWBERRY NODULES*

Land type: Desert hills.
Best season: October to April.
Tools: Rock pick, collecting bag, shovel.
Material: Agate-filled nodules.
Lore: Nodules, like geodes, were thought to be the abode of elemental spirits.
Special attraction: None.
Elevation: 1,970 feet.
Land manager: BLM.
Vehicle type: 4X4.
For more information: USGS map Newberry Springs Quadrangle.
Finding the site: Exit Interstate 40 at Memorial Drive and head west 3 miles on National Trails Highway, or exit at Newberry and head east on National Trails Highway for 2.1 miles. Turn south on Newberry Road and drive 0.6 miles. Veer right, ignoring Magnee Road. Drive 1 mile to the quarry. Even with a 4X4, you may choose to park here and walk west to the hills.

SITE 29 *NEWBERRY NODULES*

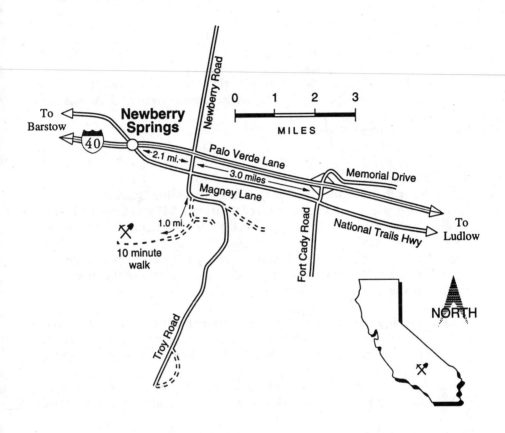

Rockhounding: By digging into the white patches of ancient ash among the hills, you will find nodules filled with agate. Some have crystalline centers. Although these are said to be rare, I have found a few over the years.

The farther into the hills you go, the better will be your luck. This area has been visited by rockhounds in past years, so plan on doing some looking and hiking about. Try to imagine where others have not looked, and you might net some nodules. It would be profitable to search in pockets that appear to have been well excavated. It is likely that not all of the nodules were recovered in the past. I have had some luck doing this.

Be prepared to do some strenuous digging in your quest for nodules or search the areas below the white deposits after heavy rains. This is a good time to find newly uncovered ones or those which have eroded out of the deposits.

SITE 30 ORBICULAR RHYOLITE AT GRANDVIEW MINE

Land type: Desert hills.
Best season: October to April.
Tools: Rock pick, collecting bag.
Material: Orbicular rhyolite.
Lore: Held during meditation, orbicular rhyolite was believed to assist in self-realization, corresponding to the adage "know thyself." This was perhaps due to the eye-like patterns.
Special attraction: None.
Elevation: 3,000 feet.
Land manager: BLM.
Vehicle type: 4X4.
For more information: USGS map Grandview Mine Quadrangle.
Finding the site: From the junction of California 247 and California 18 at Lucerne Valley, drive east 5 miles. Turn north (left) on Camp Rock Road and drive 4 miles. Veer to the right, remaining on Camp Rock Road at the fork. Drive northeast on Camp Rock Road 9 miles. Turn left and drive 1 mile. The material will be scattered on the slope faces on both sides of the road in the vicinity of the Grandview Mine.

Rockhounding: Here you will find orbicular rhyolite, so named because of the eye-like patterning. This material makes excellent display pieces and is a fine addition to any mineral collection. Less porous pieces make spectacular cabochons.

Rhyolite is a type of igneous extrusive rock. It is composed of feldspar, quartz, and amphibole often with a few other elements that affect coloration.

The Grandview Mine is aptly named. The view from there is grand, indeed. Be sure to be cautious, as there are some vertical shafts in the mine area.

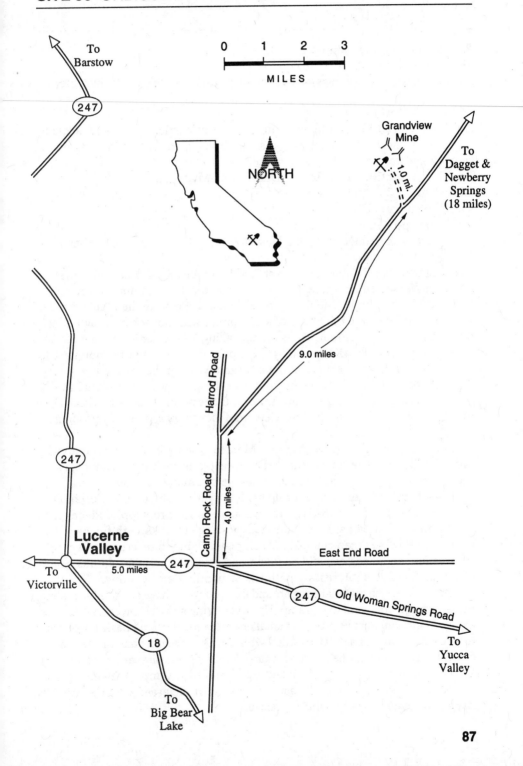

SITE 31 *MARBLE QUARRY OFF STODDARD WELL ROAD*

Land type: Desert mountain.
Best season: October to May.
Tools: Heavy canvas bags or canvas tarp, pick, chisel, crack hammer or sledge.
Material: Marble.
Lore: Greeks and European alchemists wore or carried a chip of marble to hasten healing of broken bones and skin ailments, and for its calming qualities. Makes an excellent "worry stone."
Special attraction: Roy Rogers/Dale Evans Museum.
Elevation: 4,200 feet.
Land manager: BLM.
Vehicle type: Any.
For more information: BLM's Desert Access Guide Stoddard Valley #10; USGS map Stoddard Quadrangle.
Finding the site: Exit Interstate 15 at Stoddard Wells Road. Head northeast on Stoddard Wells Road for 3 miles. When you cross the tracks continue on Stoddard Wells Road for an additional 6.8 miles. Take the dirt road to the right 1.3 miles to the base of the large mountain. The mountain will show obvious lighter-colored tailings near its summit. These are the tailings of the Verde Antique Marble Quarry. If you have a 4X4, you may drive part of the way up the mountain to the marble quarry. If not, park at the base and walk up the road to the quarry. The road has been partially washed out over the years. When I visited in early 1994, I was able to drive about one-third of the way up. The walk is about 0.3 miles. It wasn't a hard walk, and the view from the quarry is positively panoramic.

Rockhounding: The Verde Antique Marble Quarry has long been a well-known collecting site for rockhounds interested in making bookends, carvings, or other projects that require sizeable chunks of marble.

The quarry was renowned for its brilliant yellowish green material. Due to its popularity, the yellowish green marble is in rare supply. Pieces fist-sized and smaller can still be found, as can large chunks with flecks of the popular yellowish green coloring. Much material in white, cream, gray, pale green, pink, and black can still be found and occurs in sizeable chunks. Some of the material has interesting patterns of banding and veining.

There is so much material lying around that you won't have any trouble finding the size chunk you want to work up. However, bring a chisel and crack hammer along should you decide you want smaller pieces for the walk back to your vehicle. Heavy canvas bags can be filled with chunks of marble and dragged back down the mountain. A heavy canvas tarp would serve a similar purpose.

While on the mountain, I picked up a beautiful lump of jewelry-grade hematite. Although hematite wasn't abundant in the area, you may want to keep your eyes to the ground for some.

The marble quarry (white patch) near Stoddard Well on a stormy, rainy day.

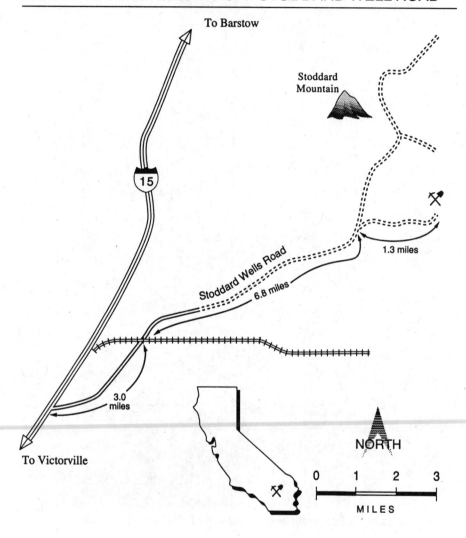

To Barstow

Stoddard Mountain

15

Stoddard Wells Road
6.8 miles

1.3 miles

3.0 miles

To Victorville

NORTH

0   1   2   3
MILES

SITE 32 *OPAL MOUNTAIN OPAL AND AGATE*

Land type: Desert mountains.
Best season: October to May.
Tools: Rock pick, collecting bag, chisel.
Material: Colorful common opal and agate.
Lore: Common opal was carried or worn to increase one's self-esteem. It was thought by increasing self-esteem, that all else would follow, such as wealth, love, and contentment.

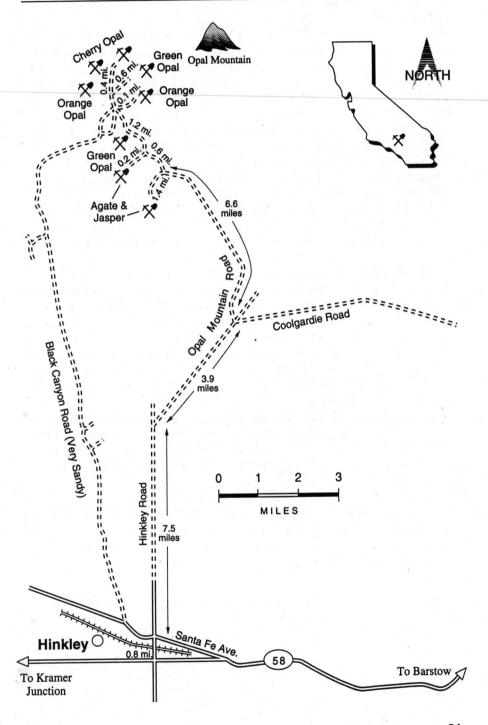

Cherry Opal

Green Opal

Opal Mountain

Orange Opal

NORTH

0.6 mi.

0.4 mi.

0.1 mi.

Orange Opal

Orange Opal

1.2 mi.

Green Opal

0.6 mi.

0.2 mi.

1.4 mi.

Agate & Jasper

6.6 miles

Opal Mountain Road

Coolgardie Road

Black Canyon Road (Very Sandy)

3.9 miles

Hinkley Road

0   1   2   3

MILES

7.5 miles

Hinkley

Santa Fe Ave.

58

0.8 mi.

To Kramer Junction

To Barstow

Special attraction: None.
Elevation: 3,800 feet.
Land manager: BLM.
Vehicle type: 4X4.
For more information: USGS map Opal Mountain Quadrangle.
Finding the site: Exit County 58 at Hinkley Road. Drive north on Hinkley Road 0.8 miles. Cross the tracks and continue another 7.5 miles. Veer northeast (right) on Opal Mountain Road and drive 3.9 miles. Take the left-most fork, staying on Opal Mountain Road. Drive another 6.6 miles. Turn left and drive 1.4 miles to gather some jasper.

Return to the 1.4-mile mark to the main northwest road (Opal Mountain Road) and continue another 0.6 miles. Turn left and drive 0.2 miles to collect more jasper and agate if you wish. Return to the 0.6-mile mark, to the main road, and go another 1.2 miles in a northwest direction. Turn right, park, and search the area for orange opal and more agate.

Return to the main road and drive 0.1 miles northwest, ignoring all roads heading left. The road straightens to almost due north. From here most roads heading to the right and left will lead to deposits of orange or green opal.

Rockhounding: Although in years past this site could be entered by two-wheel-drive vehicles, several years ago I and the members of the Bear Gulch Rock Club became hopelessly mired in deep sand. My motorhome, a couple trailers, and a large fifth-wheel were stuck fast. Even the 4X4 tow vehicle, dispatched from Barstow, that came to assist us, became mired. Finally, our most welcome escape was the result of a BLM ranger who towed each and every one of us out, including the tow truck, with his Dodge Ram Charger.

Therefore, I recommend a 4X4 or go in a group consisting of at least one 4X4 and a good tow rope.

The material is colorful common opal in orange, red, green, yellow, and white. Although it doesn't have the fire attributed to precious opal, it does seem to be "fired" with an inner glow. It occurs in seams in the mountain country rock. Yes, you will need to do some chisel work. Be careful though, this material is easily fractured.

If you find the red opal, you will be collecting the rare cherry opal. It can, with careful looking, still be collected at the northernmost collecting areas, but it is rare and usually found only in very thin seams.

SITE 33 *ONYX AND BORATE MINERALS IN MULE CANYON*

Land type: Desert mountains.
Best season: October to May.
Tools: Bag, rock pick.
Material: Translucent, honey and gray banded onyx, and borate minerals.
Lore: Romans wore onyx for protection during night travels and in battle, also to lessen libidinous desires and to calm worries. Egyptian and New Age beliefs assert that borates balance body systems and aid in maintaining skeletal strength, while ulexite enhances psychic sight.
Special attraction: Calico Ghost Town.
Elevation: 2,600 feet.
Land manager: BLM.
Vehicle type: Any.
For more information: BLM's Desert Access Guide Johnson Valley #11; USGS map Yermo Quadrangle.
Finding the site: Exit Interstate 15 at Ghost Town Road. Head north and follow the signs to Calico 3.4 miles. Past the turnoff to the gate to Calico, the road becomes Calico Road. Pass Calico Ghost Town and continue 1.9 miles to Mule Canyon Road. The road to Mule Canyon is marked with a white post, and with some squinting, one can still barely read that this is indeed the road to Mule Canyon. Turn left and drive 1.5 miles keeping right. Go an additional 0.4 plus miles, still keeping to your right. Continue another 1.6 miles in an easterly direction, ignoring the road to the right. When you see the large gray tailings pile, turn right into the wash. If you are in a two-wheel-drive vehicle, you may choose to park prior to driving into the narrow shallow wash. Parts of this wash are very sandy. After about 500 feet, the wash becomes extremely narrow and peters out.

Rockhounding: Up the wash from the gray tailings pile, 20 feet or so, and on the other side of the road, beautiful translucent chunks of onyx can be found. Some are beige and unremarkable, but the honey-colored onyx with gray, brown, and black banding is exquisite and would make beautiful jewelry and carvings. Onyx takes a high polish and has a satiny smooth feel when finished. Perhaps this is why onyx is made into "worry stones," those fifty-cent-sized pieces with thumbprint-sized depressions for carrying about in the pocket and rubbing when feeling anxious or stressed.

On the gray tailings pile in the wash, and on the other side of the wash, small specimens of borate minerals, ulexite, and colemanite (TV rock) are found.

Driving into Mule Canyon you will marvel at the coloring of the surrounding hills. The mineralization of the area creates this peculiar coloring of green, yellow, and maroon. You may want to take your camera in order to capture this unusual coloration. Miners, seeing this atypical coloring, prospected the area in the late 1800s. Silver and gold were mined until the 1920s,

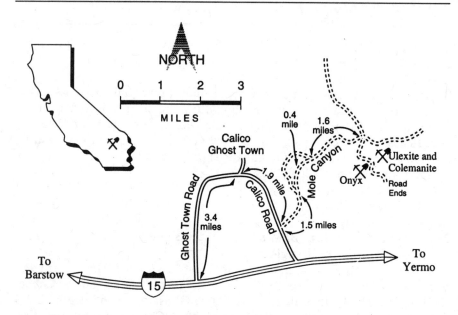

when the miners began to drift off to richer digs. Calico was restored by Walter Knott of Knottsberry Farm fame. Not only was Walter Knott an entrepreneur, but he worked the Calico mines in the year 1910. When you see the vari-colored hills, you will understand how Calico earned her name, for the hills are as colorful as a calico quilt.

There is a fee to tour the old town of Calico. Admission for adults and youngsters thirteen years and up is five dollars. For kids under 13 admission is two dollars.

Clapp Spring, a natural oasis, between Opal Hill fire agate mine and Thumb Peak near the Mule Mountains in the Southern California desert.

SITE 34 *HILLTOP AGATE AND JASPER AT MINEOLA ROAD*

Land type: Desert hills.
Best season: October to May.
Tools: Rock bag, pick.
Material: Colorful translucent agate and red jasper.
Lore: Greeks and Romans wore agate for protection, strength, and courage. Jasper was worn more to aid one in breaking bad habits, while it was used by American Indians in rain-making rites.
Special attraction: Early Man Site.
Elevation: 2,100 feet.
Land manager: BLM.
Vehicle type: Any.
For more information: BLM's Desert Access guides for Johnson Valley #11 and Irwin #8; USGS map Yermo Quadrangle.
Finding the site: Exit Interstate 15 at Mineola Road. Turn right and drive 0.6 miles. Take a well-graded dirt road north. It will be marked with a sign for the Early Man Site and the county dump. Drive north several hundred feet to the end of the road. Take the faint dirt road to the left 0.2 miles to the top of the hill next to the dump. The road to the top of the hill is rocky, and it is recommended that two-wheel-drive vehicles ascend the hill in low gear, or you may walk up the hill.

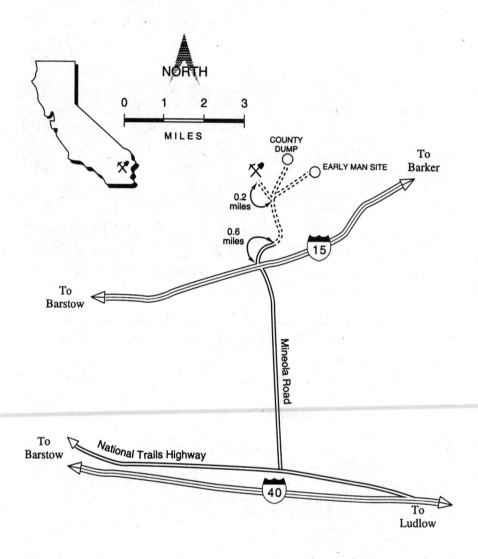

Rockhounding: This site is right off the freeway and easy to get to. The agate found at this location comes in most colors and is generally about fist-size. Red jasper in various shades abounds, as well as an occasional chalcedony rose. If you visit the agate location Wednesday through Saturday, you may wish to stop at the Early Man archeological site. Between 9 A.M. and 4 P.M. you can see some of the tools and other artifacts crafted by the ancient humans who lived in this area as early as the Pleistocene Age.

SITE 35 ALVORD MINE COPPER MINERALS AND CALCITE

Land type: Desert hills.
Best season: October to April.
Tools: Rock pick, collecting bag, chisel, shovel or rake.
Material: Chrysocolla, malachite, calcite crystals.
Lore: Chrysocolla, held in the palm of the hand, was thought to alleviate fear and bring peace. If danger threatened, it was believed that malachite would break into pieces, thereby warning its owner. Calcite was worn during fasting to aid cleansing of the body.
Special attraction: None.
Elevation: 3,900 feet.
Land manager: BLM.
Vehicle type: Any.
For more information: USGS maps Alvord Mountain East and Alvord Mountain West quadrangles.
Finding the site: From Highway 40 or Yermo Road, take Alvord Road northwest for 2.7 miles. Pass under the powerline and continue another 2.7 miles. Ignore the road to the right and drive another 0.8 miles. Turn right and go 0.4 miles to the mine.

Rockhounding: On the dumps of the old Alvord Mine you can find chrysocolla and malachite suitable for displaying and adding to mineral collections. Dig into the dumps and you may net small pieces suitable for lapidary work.

Calcite crystals in white, and with a bluish tint, may be found on the dumps and in seams on boulders. Agate, hematite, petrified wood, and jasper may also be collected in the area.

The Alvord gold mine is currently not in operation and hasn't been for many years, but that may change should the price of gold rise and the costs of production drop.

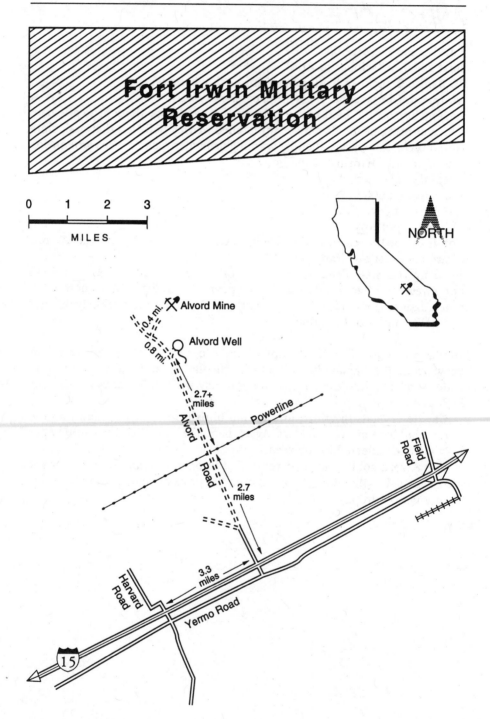

Fort Irwin Military Reservation

0 1 2 3
MILES

NORTH

Alvord Mine

0.4 mi.

0.8 mi.

Alvord Well

2.7+ miles

Powerline

Alvord Road

2.7 miles

3.3 miles

Field Road

Harvard Road

Yermo Road

15

SITE 36 *FIELD ROAD AGATES*

Land type: Desert.
Best season: October to May.
Tools: Collecting bag.
Material: Colorful small agate.
Lore: While worn for courage and protection by many ancient cultures, jasper (particularly green jasper) was worn by Egyptians for its healing properties, especially of the digestive tract.
Special attraction: None.
Elevation: 1,600 feet.
Land manager: BLM.
Vehicle type: Any.
For more information: USGS maps Alvord East and Dunn quadrangles.
Finding the site: This site consists of two locations on the opposite sides of Interstate 15, both off of Field Road, which we will label as Location A and Location B.

Location A is south of Field Road. To get there exit Interstate 15 and head slightly southeast 0.1 miles to a dirt road. Turn right onto this dirt road and head 0.2 miles into the desert to a small desert varnish-covered mound. Another 0.3 miles farther you will come to another small mound. Both these areas are covered with tumbler-size pieces of agate in gray, white, brown, and cream, some with black banding.

Jasper from Field Road.

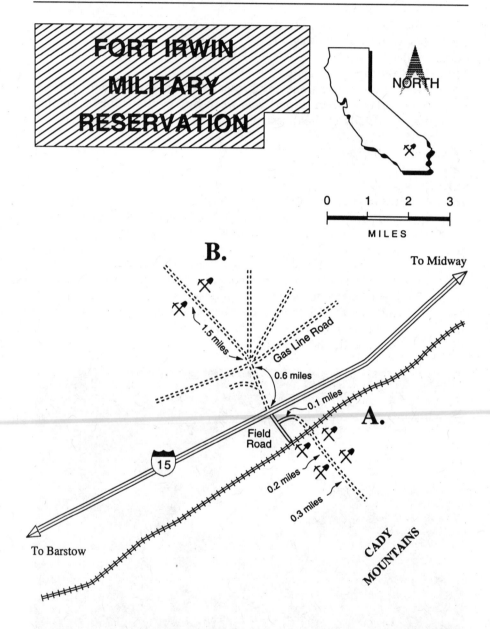

On the opposite side of the freeway is Location B, an agate area that you may want to spend more time enjoying. In fact take a picnic lunch and your camera. To get to this site exit Interstate 15 and head northwest 0.6 miles, staying right until you get to a gas line road. Here the road forks three ways. Take the left fork and drive 1.5 miles to the top of a large mound.

Rockhounding: At Location A, along with the tumbler-size agates, small pieces of red jasper and petrified wood can be found. This is a good quick trip for tumbling rough to make the kids happy. It is also a quick and convenient stop to make on the way to or from Las Vegas.

Location B is covered with palm-size pieces of translucent agate in brown, tan, cream, and white, as well as varying shades of green. I also found some nice pieces of green and red jasper. Red jasper is plentiful here. Oddly, I also found one, and only one, nice piece of fire agate. I suspect that some rockhound visiting the site must have accidently dropped it.

Pack a picnic lunch to this site and plan to spend some time enjoying the view of vast open spaces and distant mountain ranges. Bring a camera; the view is spectacular. There is no shade here, so plan to picnic in the shade created by your vehicle or plan brunch instead of lunch to take advantage of cooler morning temperatures. The desert varnished rock at this site is thick and at first appears to obscure from view the lovely agates to be found here. Within moments your eyes will become accustomed to seeing the agate and jasper against the black, varnished rocks.

SITE 37 *AFTON CANYON COLLECTIBLES*

Land type: Desert canyons.
Best season: October to May.
Tools: Pick, collecting bag.
Material: Red and yellow jasper, agate, opalite, calcite rhombs.
Lore: Opalite is reputed to have protective as well as calming qualities.

Afton Canyon.

SITE 37 *AFTON CANYON COLLECTIBLES*

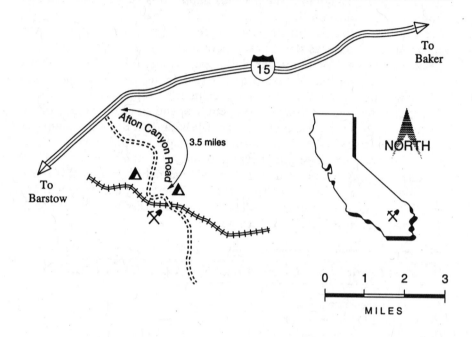

Special attraction: Afton Canyon geography.
Elevation: 1,600 feet.
Land manager: BLM.
Vehicle type: Any.
For more information: BLM's Desert Access guides for Johnson Valley #11 and Irwin #8; USGS maps Dunn and Cave Mountain quadrangles.
Finding the site: From Interstate 15 take Afton Canyon offramp and head southeast for 3.5 miles to the second BLM campground, which will be on your left. The collecting areas consist of three canyons opposite the BLM campground. In dry years you may walk under the train trestle, visible from camp, and ford the shallow Mojave River and head into one of three canyons. During the spring of 1994, recent and heavy rainfall caused the Mojave River to swell greatly, preventing collectors from crossing under the trestle due to a widening of the river and deep, viscous mud. Instead, collectors were required to climb 60 feet down the precipitous rock riprap that protects the railbed from erosion by the Mojave River.

Once down we were able to walk northwest about 200 feet to where the river narrowed and some well-placed boulders allowed for a dry crossing. The brush on the canyon side of the Mojave River is impenetrable and must be circumnavigated. This will bring you to face the center and largest of the canyons. All three canyons are reportedly good for collecting, and rockhounds have their favorites. My favorite is the center canyon.

Rockhounding: In years past rockhounds could drive (a 4X4 only) across the shallow Mojave River right into the canyon. Due to environmental destruction by ORVs, the BLM has fenced off the canyons to vehicles. You can walk into the canyons, however. After the long, hot desert summer the river may shrink back to its usual width, and much of the mud will dry, once again allowing easier access under the trestle.

If you elect to take this trip, plan to camp in the BLM campground on the east side of Afton Canyon Road. This campground is closest to the collecting site and affords covered picnic tables, an outhouse, barbecues, and numerous RV and tent camping sites. Bring ample water. This is a dry camp. At the time of my visit in 1994, there was a minimal charge of four dollars per night with a Golden Age discount of two dollars.

The geology of the area is varied and interesting. The canyons of the collecting area are of compacted mud and sand that, through erosion, have been carved into fanciful spires and minarets. Be sure to take your camera into the canyon to capture the interesting natural formations.

Abundant collecting material is found in the main canyon, but hiking the narrow side cuts yields more varied and abundant material.

The material at this site consists of red and yellow jasper, agate, opalite in pastel shades of pink and pistachio green, and occasional calcite rhombs. I also found half of a nodule filled with finger-size quartz crystals, but could find no more. Plan to visit the other two canyons, as some rockhounds claim these for their favorite collecting areas.

It is reported that a barite deposit is somewhere in the area. I have yet to locate it. Hematite is also supposed to be found in the canyon right behind the campground, although no other collectibles have been found there. Besides your camera, take a lunch or snack and drinking water. The hike to the canyon is not a long one, but the canyon and its narrow side ravines are so interesting that you may be likely to wander about for hours just looking and exploring. One day in the spring 1994 I spent a lovely day collecting with two other rockhounds I met at the Afton Campground. Irene was piloting her camper solo and Hal, another RVer, was an avid rockhound. The view from the top of the canyon is spectacular.

SITE 38 *TURQUOISE AT OLD TOLTEC MINE*

Land type: Desert hills.
Best season: October to April.
Tools: Rock pick, collecting bag, chisel, rake, shovel, screen
Material: Turquoise.
Lore: Turquoise is the sacred stone of the American Indians because of its protective and healing qualities.
Special attraction: None.
Elevation: 4,400 feet.
Land manager: BLM.

SITE 38 *TURQUOISE AT OLD TOLTEC MINE*

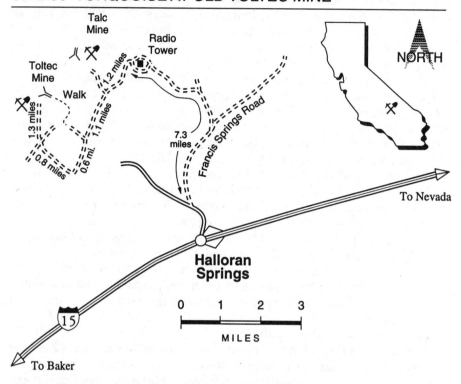

Vehicle type: High-clearance two-wheel-drive vehicle or 4X4.

For more information: USGS map Turquoise Mountain Quadrangle.

Finding the site: From Interstate 15 exit at Halloran Springs. Drive north, veering right at Francis Springs Road, for a total of 7.3 miles. Keep to the left and drive up toward the radio tower. Do not go up to the tower, but continue on the southwest road for 1.2 miles. (Ignore the road to your right.) Drive an additional 1.1 miles on the southwest road, then turn northwest (right) and drive 0.2 miles. Stop here and walk the half mile northwest to the mine. If you have a 4X4, you may wish to attempt the road to the mine, following the mileages on the map.

Rockhounding: This is the only turquoise collecting site I know of that is available to the public in California. The pieces are generally small and would be most suitable for "channel-work" jewelry. Use a rake or garden cultivator to dig through the tailings piles. A shovel would be useful for digging deeper into the tailings to access the sky blue material overlooked by previous collectors. A fine-mesh screen, one quarter inch, would also be useful in screening out turquoise pieces.

The old tunnel workings are unsafe to enter, so confine your collecting to tailings piles, gullies, and washes.

SITE 39 *CLARK MOUNTAIN COPPER AND LEAD MINERALS*

Land type: Desert hills.
Best season: October to April.
Tools: Rock pick, collecting bag, chisel, shovel.
Material: Azurite, chrysocolla, malachite, smithsonite, galena, sphalerite.
Lore: Copper minerals of all types and smithsonite aid in meditation and development of the "psychic body." Galena was thought to "ground" one emotionally and balance the body functions. Sphalerite was carried to protect one against treachery, enabling its owner to recognize it by intuition.
Special attraction: None.
Elevation: 3,900 feet.
Land manager: BLM.
Vehicle type: 4X4.
For more information: USGS map Mescal Range Quadrangle.
Finding the site: Exit Interstate 15 at Cima Road. Drive 0.7 miles north, then turn right and drive 4.1 miles east. Turn north (left) and continue 0.7 miles. Turn right and drive a short distance to the Mohawk Mine.

SITE 39 *CLARK MOUNTAIN COPPER AND LEAD MINERALS*

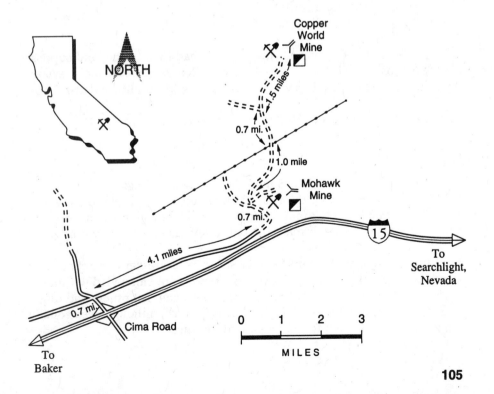

To get to the Copper World Mine, return the short distance from the Mohawk Mine, turning right and continuing 1 mile farther north, ignoring the road to the left. Cross the powerline road and continue 0.7 miles. Ignore the road to the left and drive an additional 1.5 miles to the Copper World Mine.

Rockhounding: The numerous dumps of the Mohawk Mine provide mineral collectors with nice metallic specimens of galena and resinous-looking sphalerite. Keep an eye open for occasional specimens of smithsonite, which crystallize in the botryoidal form usually as a coating on other rocks.

The Copper World Mine is a great spot for collecting fine specimens of the copper minerals of azurite, malachite, and chrysocolla. My friend, Herman, found a fabulous palm-size piece of chrysocolla there recently.

The Copper World Mine was open to rockhounds on my last visit, but it does go through spates of re-opening for production, which closes it to rockhound access every time new gem material is discovered. When the vein of new gem material pinches out, the mine is then shut down and made available again for rockhounding.

SITE 40 *OLD ZABRISKIE STATION PRECIOUS OPAL*

Land type: Desert hills.
Best season: October to April.
Tools: Rock pick, collecting bag.
Material: Opal.
Lore: Today's superstitions consider opal a "bad-luck" stone, and supposedly only those born in October may wear it. However, the ancients revered opal and believed it aided its wearer in attaining invisibility and astral projection.
Special attraction: Death Valley National Park.
Elevation: 1,300 feet.
Land manager: BLM.
Vehicle type: Any.
For more information: USGS map Ibex Pass Quadrangle.
Finding the site: From California 127 take the road opposite the ruins of Zabriskie Station west 0.2 miles. Hunt the opal by digging among the hills and mud cliffs or going through the tailings of digging done by others.

Rockhounding: Opal is found in small stringers inside clay concretions that weather out of the mud cliffs. These concretions are embedded within the cliffs. I had my best luck digging where I saw signs that others had dug.

The opal is generally too thin for lapidary work, although occasionally larger pieces have been found by patient hunting.

SITE 40 *OLD ZABRISKIE STATION PRECIOUS OPAL*
SITE 41 *SPERRY WASH FOSSILS, PETRIFIED WOOD, AND AGATE*

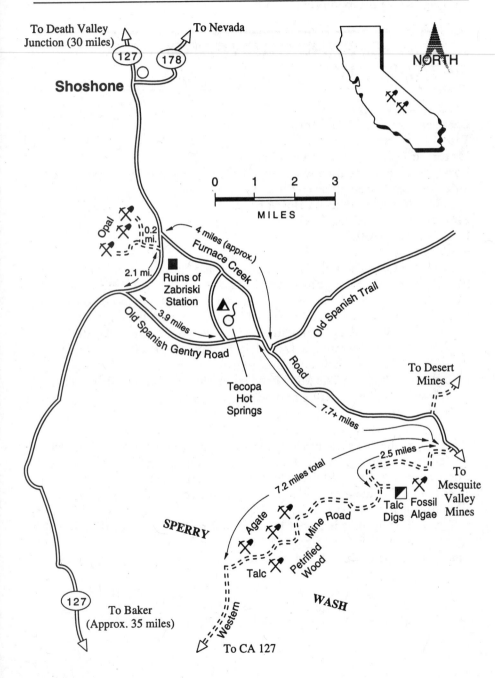

To Death Valley Junction (30 miles)

To Nevada

127

178

Shoshone

NORTH

0   1   2   3
MILES

Opal

0.2 mi.

4 miles (approx.)

Furnace Creek

2.1 mi.

Ruins of Zabriski Station

3.9 miles

Old Spanish Gentry Road

Old Spanish Trail

Road

Tecopa Hot Springs

To Desert Mines

7.7+ miles

2.5 miles

To Mesquite Valley Mines

7.2 miles total

Agate

Mine Road

Talc Digs

Fossil Algae

SPERRY

Talc

Petrified Wood

Western

WASH

127

To Baker (Approx. 35 miles)

To CA 127

107

In the rockhound classic *Gem Trails of California*, by James R. Mitchell, an agate and chalcedony rose collecting spot is mentioned. This is 24 miles farther north of Zabriskie Station on CA 127. Look on both sides of the road for scattered agate with orange banding and white chalcedony roses. I have not visited this agate and rose spot, but it might be a thought, should the opal digs prove disappointing.

SITE 41 *SPERRY WASH FOSSILS, PETRIFIED WOOD, AND AGATE*

Land type: Desert.
Best season: October to April.
Tools: Rock pick, collecting bag, chisel.
Material: Fossils, petrified wood, agate.
Lore: Fossils and petrified wood were believed to insure their owners with long life. Agate brought strength and courage and was worn in battle.
Special attraction: Tecopa Hot Springs.
Elevation: 1,750 feet.
Land manager: BLM.
Vehicle type: 4X4.
For more information: USGS maps Tecopa and Tecopa Dunes quadrangles.
Finding the site: From Interstate 127, near the ruins of Zabriskie Station, turn east on Furnace Creek Road. Drive approximately 4 miles southeast. Stay on Furnace Creek Road where it branches right, away from the Old Spanish Trail Road. Drive an additional 7.7 miles. Turn right on Western Talc Mine Road. Drive 2.5 miles and turn left, heading to the talc mine. Here you can collect talc specimens and fossil algae.

Back out to Western Talc Mine Road go another 4.7 miles farther. Between the talc mine and here, agate and petrified wood may be gathered on both sides of the road.

Rockhounding: This site has long been a favorite of rockhounds. The fossils are located to the east of the talc pit in the limestone cliffs. The petrified wood and agate are still fairly plentiful, even after decades of collecting.

Although the talc mine is currently inoperative, it is advisable to respect all no-trespassing signs.

Tecopa Hot Springs is a spot to camp and relax after a rockhound trip. There are several RV campgrounds in the area, where one can soak away aches and pains in the mineral-rich waters.

SITE 42 *GEM HILL AGATE, RHYOLITE, AND COMMON OPAL*

Land type: Desert Hills.
Best season: October to May.
Tools: Rock pick, collecting bag, shovel.
Material: Agate, rhyolite, common opal.
Lore: Agate brings courage and strength. Rhyolite is the stone of "self-realization," and common opal was thought to enhance wealth and relationships by increasing one's self-esteem.
Special attraction: Tropico Gold Mine tour.
Elevation: 2,800 feet.
Land manager: BLM.
Vehicle type: Any.
For more information: USGS map Soledad Mountain Quadrangle.
Finding the site: From California 14 exit at Rosamond Boulevard and head west 3.2 miles to Mojave-Tropico Road. Turn north (right) and drive 4.6 miles. Turn left. Just about any spot to the right or left of the road, from where it turns off of Mojave-Tropico Road, is a good place to find agate, or follow the mileages indicated on the map.

Rockhounding: This has always been one of my favorite sites for collecting agate. The agate occurs in a variety of colors and patterns, as does the rhyolite. Near the Tropico Gold Mine, much of the rhyolite contains clear, quartz crystals. The petrified wood occurs in green and white, and most of the common opal found is green or white.

Look on the flats and hills adjacent to the road and dig into the greenish deposits.

The Tropico Gold Mine tour is interesting. The tour guide will take you through part of the mine and mill and explain the mechanics of gold mining. Although there are no plans to re-open the Tropico, there was some discussion of re-opening the mill for processing ore shipped in from other mines. The tour is run by the family that owns the mine, and the hours vary. There is a small fee for the tour.

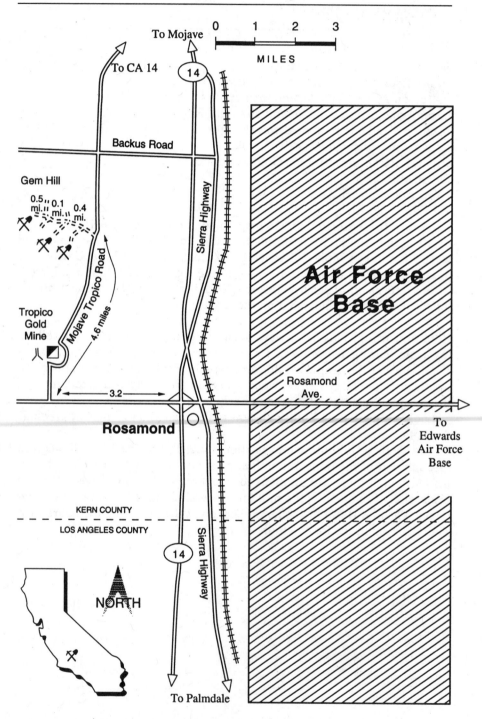

To Mojave

0   1   2   3
MILES

To CA 14

14

Backus Road

Sierra Highway

Gem Hill

0.5 mi. 0.1 mi. 0.4 mi.

Air Force Base

Mojave Tropico Road

4.6 miles

Tropico Gold Mine

3.2

Rosamond Ave.

Rosamond

To Edwards Air Force Base

KERN COUNTY

LOS ANGELES COUNTY

14

Sierra Highway

NORTH

To Palmdale

SITE 43 *SAN GABRIEL RIVER GOLD*

Land type: Inland mountains.
Best season: Year-round.
Tools: Gold pan, sluice box, shovel, pick, buckets.
Material: Gold.
Lore: Gold symbolizes wealth and wisdom and is used to alleviate arthritis pain.
Special attraction: Follow's Camp Mining Museum.
Elevation: 7,000 feet.
Land manager: USDAFS.
Vehicle type: Any.
For more information: USGS map Glendora Quadrangle; Camp Williams, 818-910-1126; Follow's Camp, 818-910-1100; USDAFS 818-335-1251.
Finding the site: From Interstate 210 take the Azusa Boulevard offramp (California 39) and drive north toward the mountains for 2.8 miles. Drive up into the mountains for 8.9 miles to East Fork Road. Turn right on East Fork Road, which crosses the San Gabriel River below. Continue another 4 miles to Camp Williams Restaurant and campground. You may prospect for gold anywhere from Camp Williams to the end of the road at Heaton Flat.

Rockhounding: Flakes of gold and an occasional nugget may be found along the banks of the San Gabriel River between the Camp Williams Restaurant and Heaton Flat at the end of the road. Panning and sluicing are allowed

Author's nephew, Perry Butler, grins at the gold he finds in his sluice box.

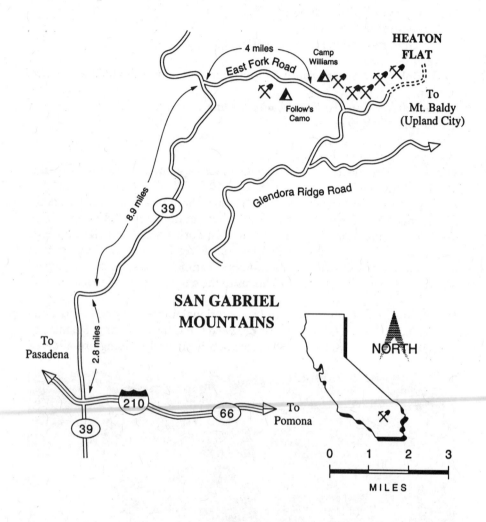

along the river. Motorized equipment, such as suction dredges and highbankers, require permits and are subject to restrictions. It is best to call the USDA Forest Service for current regulations concerning motorized equipment.

A knowledge of how to use a gold pan and sluice box is helpful. While gold is found along the river all season long, the best time is after a heavy rainfall when gold will be more abundant.

Look for concentrations of gold on the downstream sides of large rocks and boulders, among tree roots at the water's edge, and at the inside curves or bends in the river, sand bars, and where water flow is slowed.

Tent and RV camping is available at Camp Williams and nearby Follow's Camp. You may prospect for gold at Follow's Camp if you are camping there. A small store at Follow's Camp, owned by Mr. and Mrs. Marconi, sells some prospecting equipment and occasionally offers gold prospecting classes. The mining museum at Follow's Camp is interesting to see and has information on the historic southern California gold rush. While gold is found at Follow's Camp, I personally have found more gold farther up river beyond Camp Williams.

It is advisable, if you wish to camp at either of these campgrounds, to call ahead for reservations, especially during the summer season. On weekends and holidays a three dollar parking permit is required to park along the San Gabriel River. You may purchase one at a kiosk at the base of the mountains or at the Camp Williams Restaurant. Good luck and good prospecting!

SITE 44 *WRIGHTWOOD ACTINOLITE*

Land type: Alpine forest.
Best season: March to October.
Tools: Rock pick, collecting bag.
Material: Actinolite, actinolite crystals.
Lore: Actinolite was believed to bring joy, luck, and wisdom.
Special attraction: None.
Elevation: 7,000 feet.
Land manager: USDAFS.
Vehicle type: Any.
For more information: USGS maps Big Pines, Mescal Creek, Mount San Antonio, and Telegraph Peak quadrangles.
Finding the site: From Interstate 15, take California 138 north to California 2 and head west. On California 2 drive approximately 4 miles to the town of Wrightwood. Pass Wrightwood, continue another 4 miles, and turn left, remaining on California 2, where County Route N4 forks to the right. Continue another 6 miles. Park and search the washes and gullies on both sides of the road.

Another location for actinolite is found turning southeast on Lone Pine Canyon Road at Wrightwood. Continue a half mile to the big wash near the road. Most washes and gullies in this area will yield bright, silvery green-bladed actinolite, as well as dense, jade green crystals.

Rockhounding: This is a good trip to take when desert temperatures reach their unbearable, summertime highs. The more massive form of actinolite, which is rather soft and composed of interlocking bladed crystals, makes a nice addition to a mineral collection and a nice display piece because of its silvery green coloration. The monoclinic prismatic crystals are hard enough for jewelry making. I've had good luck finding the crystals at the Lone Pine Canyon Road location.

This is a nice place to bring a picnic lunch. The nearby town of Wrightwood also has a couple of good pizza parlors.

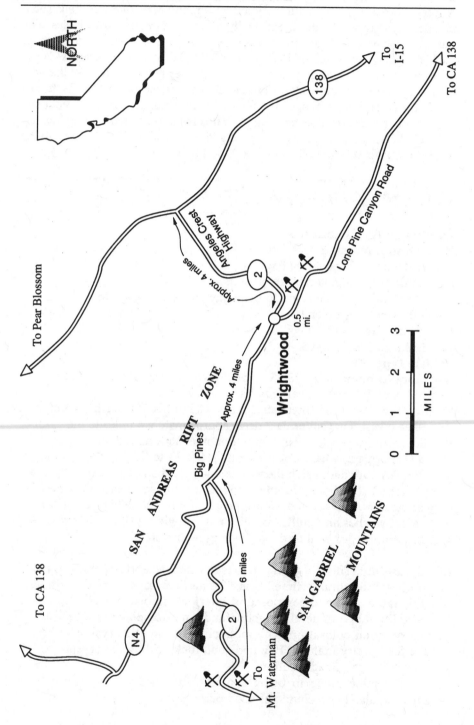

SITE 45 *IN-KO-PAH PARK ASTERATED QUARTZ AND MOONSTONE FELDSPAR*

Land type: Desert hills.
Best season: September to May.
Tools: Collecting bag, pick.
Material: Asterated quartz, moonstone feldspar, garnet.
Lore: Quartz showing inner rainbows brought hope and inspiration. Feldspar was believed to have protective qualities. In the thirteenth century garnet was worn for strength, protection, and to repel insects.
Special attraction: None.
Elevation: 1,640 feet.
Land manager: BLM.
Vehicle type: Any.
For more information: BLM's Desert Access Guide McCain Valley #19; USGS map In-Ko-Pah Gorge Quadrangle.

SITE 45 *IN-KO-PAH PARK ASTERATED QUARTZ AND MOONSTONE FELDSPAR*

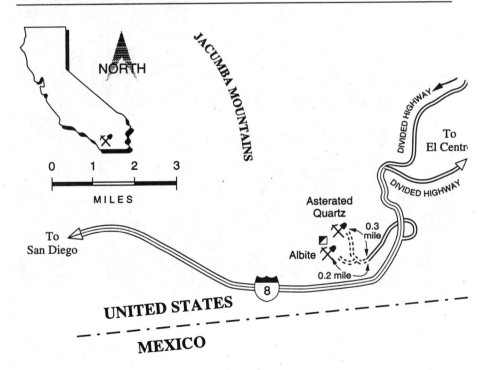

Albite "moonstone" feldspar.

Finding the site: From Interstate 8 take the In-Ko-Pah Park Road west-northwest of the highway and drive several hundred yards to its end and park. Several trails head west to the nearby hills. An easy walk west will bring you to the moonstone feldspar location. Follow the float up the rocky hill to its source. Beware of a vertical shaft farther up the hill. To reach the asterated quartz location, follow the trail from In-Ko-Pah Park Road north-west to a low hill. The quartz litters the ground at the base of the hill. Occasional garnets can be found in matrix at the quartz location.

Rockhounding: Asterated quartz, also called cats-eye quartz, when cut along one axis reveals asterism, a star-shaped optical phenomenon. Look for pieces which display flashes of rainbow color. This seems to be the best clue as to which pieces will display asterism when cut. Experimentation in cutting will be required to discover which axis displays the phenomenon. Care will be required in grinding so as to preserve asteration.

The seed- to pea-size garnets found at this location are not gem quality, but make nice specimen pieces when removed with matrix.

Moonstone feldspar, or albite, is a variety of plagioclase feldspar. Opalescence becomes pronounced when the albite is cut and polished. Again, experimentation in cutting will determine which cleavage axis most demonstrates the desired luster. The albite at this location was mined in years past for use in pottery and china production. This location is about 3 miles from the U.S.-Mexico border.

SITE 46 *COYOTE MOUNTAINS FOSSILS AND MORE*

Land type: Desert hills.
Best season: October to May.
Tools: Rock pick, collecting bag.
Material: Fossils, mica-books, black tourmaline.
Lore: Fossils guaranteed a long life. Mica was believed to protect against earthquakes; good news for us Californians! Black tourmaline, or schorl, was thought to deflect black magic.
Special attraction: None.
Elevation: 439 feet.
Land manager: BLM.
Vehicle type: Any.
For more information: USGS maps Ocotillo and Painted Gorge quadrangles.
Finding the site: From Interstate 8 take the Ocotillo exit and head 4 miles east on California S80. Turn north (left) on Painted Gorge Road. The first collecting site is 3.3 miles up Painted Gorge Road and about 300 feet to the west of the road.

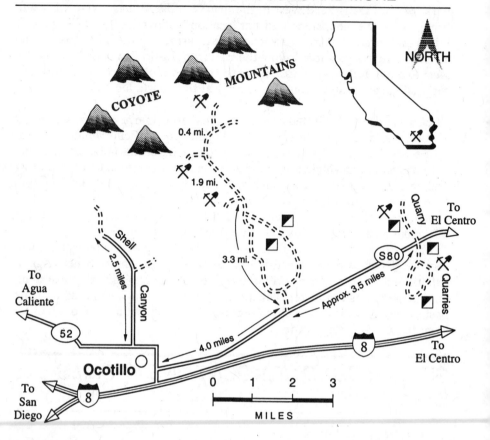

Driving another 1.9 miles farther north on Painted Gorge Road, you will come to another area to collect, but you will need a 4X4 to negotiate this road. An additional site is located 0.4 miles farther on. Turn north onto a road and park at the base of the hill. Walk up the hill and about 0.2 miles to the base of some more hills.

Rockhounding: At this site numerous types of fossil crustaceans may be collected. Also, around the gravel pits one can collect samples of muscovite and biotite mica, some with numerous sheets making up tiny "books." Black tourmaline, or schorl, may also be collected, along with occasional pink and lavender pieces of lipidolite. One may also find calcite and calcite crystals on or around the gravel pits. There are a couple campgrounds in the area where you can pitch your tent or park your RV.

Black tourmaline "schorl" in pegmatite from San Diego area. Photo by W.R.C. Shedenhelm.

SITE 47 *PATRICK'S POINT BEACH AGATES*

Land type: Coastal.
Best season: September to May.
Tools: Collecting bag.
Material: Beach-washed agate.
Lore: Agate was believed to protect its wearer from harm, both physical and occult, as well as bring courage in battle.
Special attractions: Beach recreation and camping.
Elevation: 180 feet.
Land manager: California Department of Parks and Recreation.
Vehicle type: Any.
For more information: USGS map Trinidad Quadrangle.
Finding the site: From U.S. Highway 101 take the Patrick's Point exit and head west about one-half mile to the beach at Patrick's Point State Park.

Rockhounding: This site yields beach-washed agate. When I was there last, there were restrictions on how much of the agate could be collected. Camping is available at the state park.

Winter months during low tide is the best time to collect, as well as after winter storms.

SITE 47 *PATRICK'S POINT BEACH AGATES*

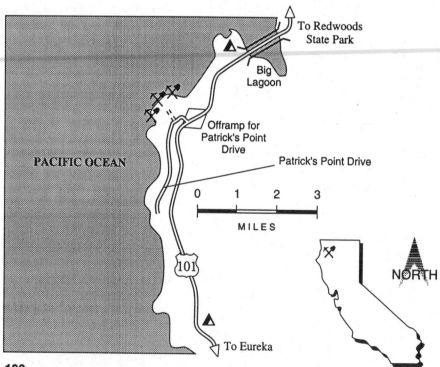

SITE 48 *AGATE BEACH JASPER, AGATE, AND PETRIFIED WOOD*

Land type: Coastal.
Best season: September to April.
Tools: Collecting bag.
Material: Oil agate, jasper, petrified wood.
Lore: Agate and Jasper were known for bringing protection and courage. Jasper was used in rituals to bring rain. Ownership of petrified wood, if agatized, would have all the attributes of agate plus help insure long life, much the same as a fossil. Also some believed that petrified wood protected against drowning, a good thing to find when beach collecting.
Special attraction: Point Reyes Bird Observatory natural history tours.
Elevation: 250 feet.
Land manager: California Department of Parks and Recreation.
Vehicle type: Any.
For more information: USGS map Bolinas Quadrangle.
Finding the site: Exit California 1 at Bolinas Road. Head southwest 1.8 miles to Mesa Road. Turn right on Mesa Road and drive 0.6 miles to Overlook Road. Turn left and drive a half mile to Elm Road and turn right. Drive 0.8 miles on Elm Road to the beach.

Rockhounding: The prize to be found here is "oil agate." This is a clear to translucent agate with dark spots. You may also find occasional pieces of petrified whale bone, as well as abalone shell. Abalone shell can be tumble polished and used in lapidary projects.

As with most coastal sites, winter months after storms are the best times to collect.

SITE 48 *AGATE BEACH JASPER, AGATE, AND PETRIFIED WOOD*

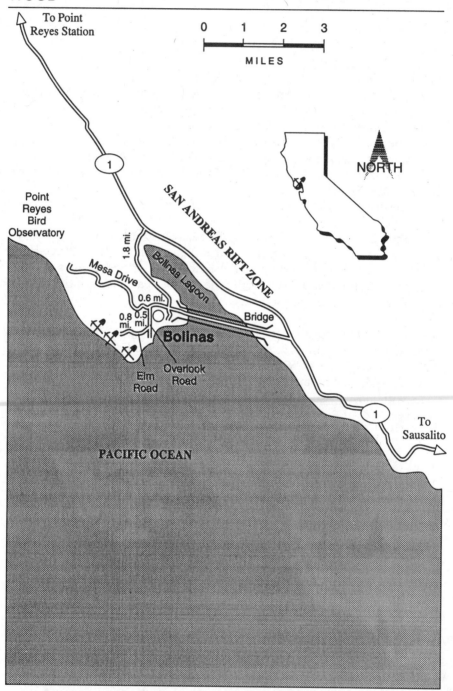

To Point
Reyes Station

0   1   2   3

MILES

NORTH

Point
Reyes
Bird
Observatory

SAN ANDREAS RIFT ZONE

1.8 mi.

Mesa Drive

Bolinas Lagoon

0.6 mi.

0.8 mi. 0.5 mi.

Bridge

Bolinas

Elm Road

Overlook Road

1

To Sausalito

PACIFIC OCEAN

SITE 49 *BEACH-WASHED JADE & ACTINOLITE AT JADE COVE*

Land type: Coastal.
Best season: October to March.
Tools: Collecting bag.
Material: Jade, actinolite.
Lore: Jade brought prosperity, luck, and wisdom to its wearer. Actinolite was thought to be similar in attribute to jade, although somewhat milder. It was also believed to assist in ridding oneself of unwanted conditions.
Special attraction: Hearst Castle near San Simeon.
Elevation: 400 feet.
Land manager: California Department of Parks and Recreation.
Vehicle type: Any.
For more information: USGS map Cape San Martin Quadrangle.
Finding the site: From California 1 exit to any of the beach locations between the town of Gorda and Plaskett Creek. All this stretch is Jade Beach.

SITE 49 *BEACH-WASHED JADE & ACTINOLITE AT JADE COVE*

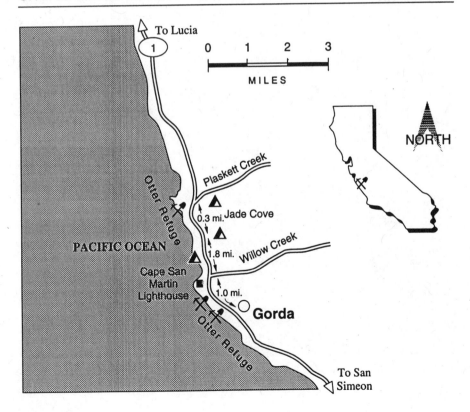

Rockhounding: This site has long been known for its beach-washed jade pebbles and boulders. This site was recently removed from collecting status. However, due to efforts by several rock clubs, this site is expected to be returned to collecting status soon. Should you decide to go to this site, be sure to obey any signs either prohibiting jade collecting or listing any restrictions.

The best time to collect here is at low tide during the winter months, especially after storms. When you collect at low tide, keep an eye on the water line. Some areas of this beach may be cut off from escape should the tide come in. Be aware of this danger and you won't have any trouble. Also, if you are taking children, watch that they do not become trapped by incoming tides.

SITE 50 *MOONSTONE BEACH*

Land type: Coastal.
Best season: November to March.
Tools: Collecting bag.
Material: Moonstones.
Lore: Moonstones have long been associated with witchcraft and goddess worship. They were believed to protect their wearer against malefic magic and enhance prophetic dreaming and psychic awareness.

Moonstone Beach. Photo by W.R.C. Shedenhelm.

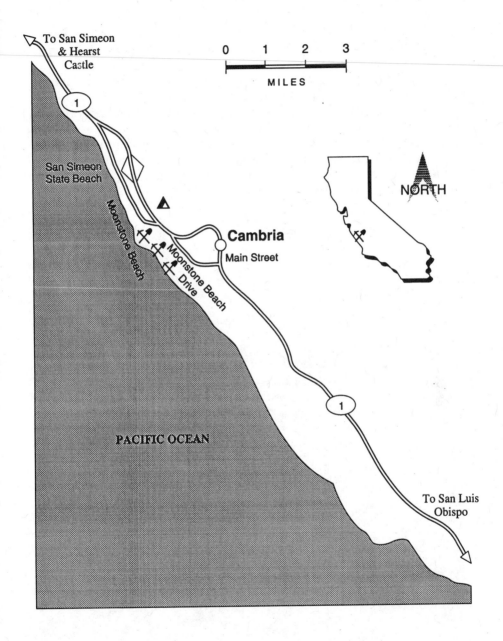

To San Simeon
& Hearst
Castle

1

0   1   2   3

MILES

San Simeon
State Beach

Moonstone Beach

Moonstone Beach Drive

Cambria

Main Street

NORTH

PACIFIC OCEAN

1

To San Luis
Obispo

Special attractions: The town of Cambria and nearby Hearst Castle.
Elevation: 500 feet.
Land manager: California Department of Parks and Recreation.
Vehicle type: Any.
For more information: USGS maps San Simeon, Pico Creek, and Cambria quadrangles.
Finding the site: From California 1 take Main Street to Moonstone Beach Drive. Moonstone Beach stretches from San Simeon to the town of Cambria.

Rockhounding: This site has long been famous for its beach-washed moonstones. Moonstone is a type of opalescent feldspar.

Camping is available at two state parks, just north of Cambria, off California 1.

Cambria is a small town with numerous artists and artisans selling their wares in small, expensive shops. Hearst Castle was one of several magnificent homes built by publishing magnate William Randolph Hearst. Tours are available by reservation.

Fossil collecting at cliff bases on Jalama Beach.

SITE 51 *JALAMA BEACH AGATE, FOSSILS, AND MARCASITE*

Land type: Coastal.
Best season: September to March.
Tools: Rock pick, collecting bag, chisels.
Material: Agate, fossils, marcasite.
Lore: Agate brought to its wearer protection and courage. Fossils insured one of long life, and marcasite, according to New Age sources, assists one in dealing with and healing co-dependency issues.
Special attractions: Jalama Beach camping and beachcombing.
Elevation: 850 feet.
Land manager: Santa Barbara County.
Vehicle type: Any.
For more information: USGS map Lompoc Hills Quadrangle.
Finding the site: From California 1, coming from Lompoc, turn right on Jalama Road at a sign indicating Jalama Beach. Be watchful, the sign is small and easily missed. If you are coming from the Buellton area, you will make a left turn onto Jalama Road. Head toward the coast through hilly, cattle country for 12 miles until you see the beach.

Rockhounding: This is a fantastic site for either tent or RV camping. One may elect to camp on the beach or high on the cliff above, where the view is fabulous. Cement pads are provided for RV beach camping. There are no hook-ups. Bring your own drinking water, as the water sources at the beach are not suitable for drinking.

Here one can find tide pools, and the beachcombing is great. Translucent rootbeer brown agate with white veining is plentiful. The sedimentary cliffs lining the beach yield fossils and marcasite, a metallic crystalline form similar to pyrite. One may also gather sea shells, abalone shells, and driftwood. Look for these other gem treasures, travertine, jade, and chert.

The beach was once the site of a Chumash Indian village. The village existed for centuries near the creek, which runs down out of the hills and across the beach into the sea. The village was left deserted when the Spanish invaders removed the Indians from their homes and took them to La Purisima Mission. The best time to collect here is off-season when winter storms and the lack of vacationers insure plentiful collecting material.

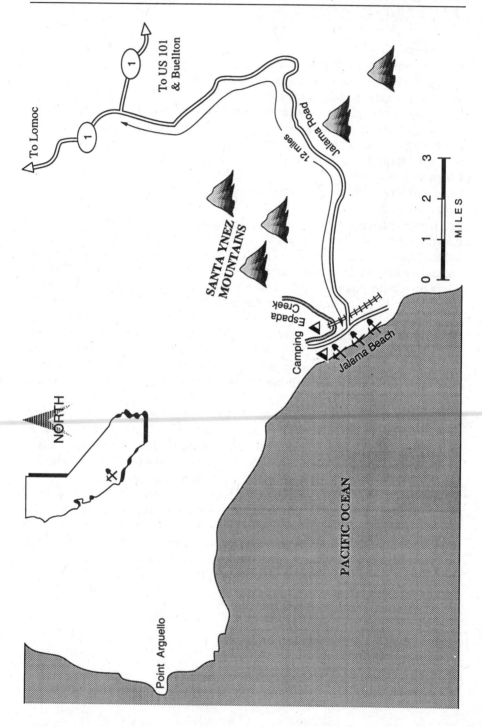

SITE 52 *GAVIOTA BEACH PETRIFIED WHALE BONE AND FOSSILS*

Land type: Coastal.
Best season: October to March.
Tools: Rock pick, collecting bag, chisel.
Material: Whale bone, fish and plant fossils.
Lore: The ancients believed that possession of a fossil insured long life.
Special attraction: Beach camping.
Elevation: 400 feet.
Land manager: California Department of Parks and Recreation.
Vehicle type: Any.
For more information: USGS map Gaviota Quadrangle.
Finding the site: From U.S. Highway 101 take the Gaviota Beach turn-off to Gaviota Beach.

Rockhounding: This site offers collecting of a variety of fossils. Camping is available here at the state campground. The best time for collecting is during the winter months. After winter storms beach-washed material, such as whale bone, is much more plentiful.

Use your rock pick and chisel to remove fossil-containing, sedimentary, cliff material.

SITE 52 *GAVIOTA BEACH PETRIFIED WHALE BONE AND FOSSILS*

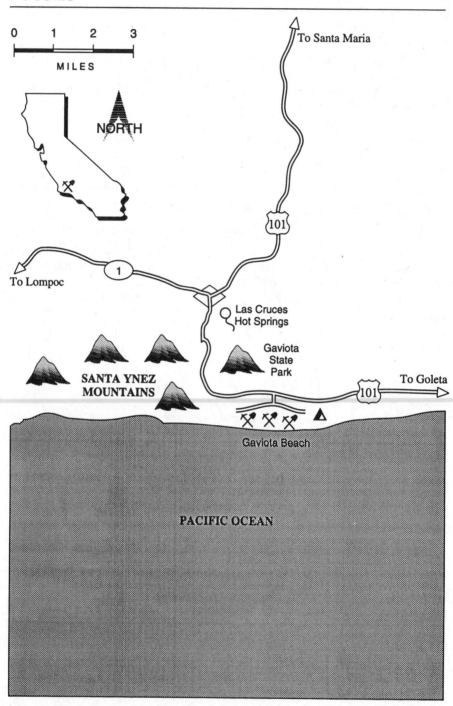

SITE 53 *SOUTHERN COAST BEACHCOMBING*

Land type: Coastal.
Best season: December to February.
Tools: Collecting bag.
Material: Beach agate, jasper.
Lore: Agate and jasper bring to their owners courage and protection. Jasper is valued by Native Americans for rain-bringing properties.
Special attractions: Beach recreation and people watching.
Elevation: 340 feet.
Land manager: Los Angeles County.
Vehicle type: Any.
For more information: USGS maps Redondo Beach and Venice Beach quadrangles. See map on p. 132.
Finding the site: From Interstate 405 take Torrance Boulevard west to Redondo Beach or El Segundo Boulevard west to El Segundo Beach. The Pacific Coast Highway runs many miles, north and south, along the coast. Most roadways crossing Pacific Coast Highway will take you west to any number of other beaches you may wish to visit.

Rockhounding: El Segundo and Hermosa beaches are collected for their ocean-tumbled, colorful agates. Redondo Beach not only has beach-washed agate, but "moonstones" as well. The Redondo Beach moonstones are actually a translucent, white agate.

These beach sites are in the busy, urban sprawl of Los Angeles County. Therefore, the best and least crowded times to collect are after winter storms bring new material up onto the beach and during winter months when cold, damp, foggy weather keeps hordes of sunbathers at home.

Most of the beaches provide barbecue pits for after-collecting picnics and barbecues.

SITE 54 *PALOS VERDES BEACH BARITE CRYSTALS*

Land type: Coastal cliffs.
Best season: Year-round.
Tools: Rock pick, collecting bag, chisel.
Material: Cockscomb barite crystals.
Lore: New Age beliefs relate that barite assists one in knowing that all things are possible.
Special attraction: Beach recreation.
Elevation: 600 feet.
Land manager: Los Angeles County.
Vehicle type: Any.

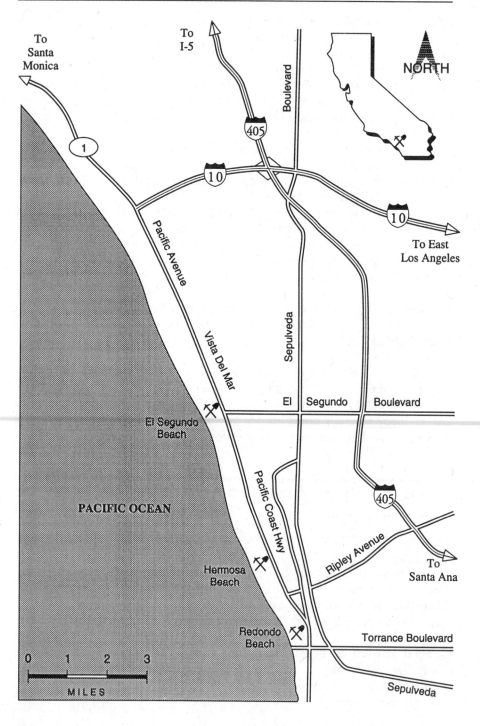

For more information: USGS maps San Pedro, Redondo Beach, and Torrance quadrangles.

Finding the site: From Interstate 405 exit on Western Avenue and head south, approximately 10 miles. Turn right on 25th street, which will become Palos Verdes Drive from here to the lighthouse, approximately 6 miles. Park your vehicle and walk down to the beach on one of the numerous paths down the cliffs. Be careful when descending to the beach. Some paths are steeper than others.

Rockhounding: At the bases of the beach cliffs below the quarry is the best area to collect barite-covered rocks, which erode out of the sea cliffs. The barite crystals are white to beige, generally translucent, and form in the cockscomb habit. They will generally fluoresce a cream color under an ultraviolet lamp. The best time to collect is during the winter months, when the beaches are basically deserted and when winter storms have eroded out the cliff material. This is also the best time to collect fossil whale bone on the beach.

Embedded in the cliffs between the lighthouse and Marineland, fossil shells may be found. These collecting areas are good ones for picnic lunches and enjoying the beach and people-watching during warmer months.

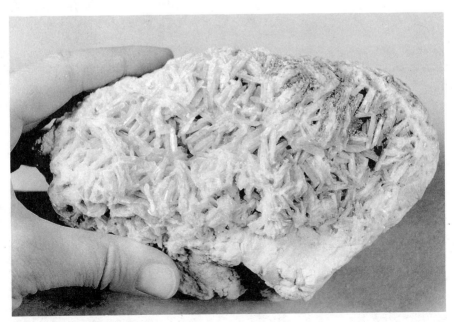

Palos Verdes barite crystals.

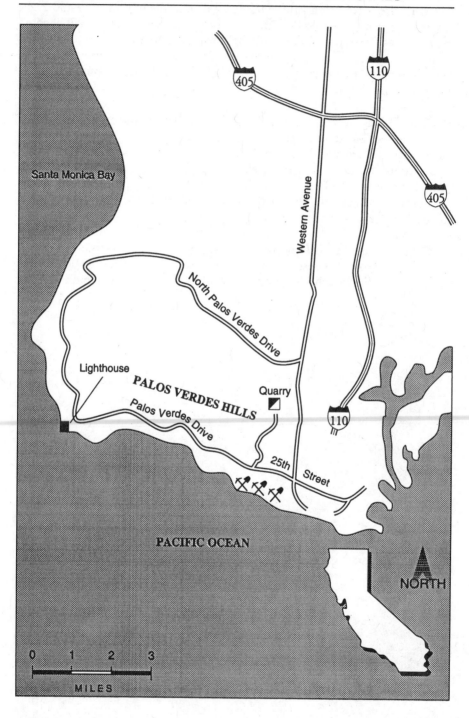

Santa Monica Bay

405

110

Western Avenue

North Palos Verdes Drive

405

Lighthouse

PALOS VERDES HILLS

Quarry

Palos Verdes Drive

110

25th Street

PACIFIC OCEAN

NORTH

0 1 2 3

MILES

SITE 55 *ANDERSON LAKE AGATE AND JASPER*

Land type: Foothills.
Best season: April to October.
Tools: Rock pick, collecting bag.
Material: Jasper, agate, magnesite.
Lore: Jasper and agate were worn for protection and courage, while jasper was used in Native American rain-bringing ceremonies. Magnesite is used during meditation to enhance visualization.
Special attraction: Rosicrucian Park in nearby San Jose.
Elevation: 1,300 feet.
Land manager: Santa Clara County.
Vehicle type: Any.
For more information: USGS maps Morgan Hill and Mount Sizer quadrangles.
Finding the site: From U.S. Highway 101, as it passes through the town of Morgan Hill, exit at either East Dunne Avenue or Cochran Avenue and head northeast 3 to 4 miles to Anderson Lake County Park. All along the lake shore colorful agate and jasper may be collected.

Rockhounding: Boating and fishing can also be enjoyed at this location. Camping is available at Henry W. Coe State Park, which is located about 12 miles northeast of Anderson Lake on East Dunne Avenue.

On the south end of the reservoir, look for blue and white agate or some which is blue and clear. At the north end look for white magnesite with reddish brown veins. Jasper is found all around. This site was contributed by two friends of mine from San Jose, George Price and Sharon Frazier.

Of further interest in nearby San Jose is Rosicrucian Park at Naglee and Park avenues, off of The Alameda Boulevard. The park takes up one city block and is home to a planetarium offering daily shows, an Egyptian museum with authentic mummies and other Egyptian, Assyrian, and Babylonian artifacts, gift shop, and espresso bar.

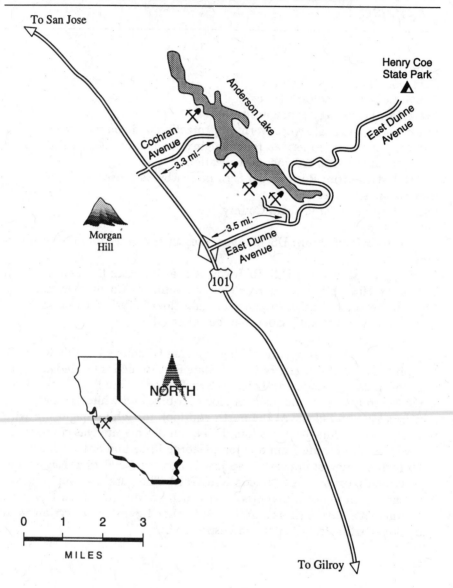

To San Jose

Henry Coe
State Park

Anderson Lake

East Dunne
Avenue

Cochran
Avenue

← 3.3 mi.

Morgan
Hill

← 3.5 mi. →

East Dunne
Avenue

101

NORTH

MILES

0   1   2   3

To Gilroy

SITE 56 *MOTHER LODE MARIPOSITE*

Land type: Oak-covered hills.
Best season: April to October.
Tools: Rock pick, collecting bag, chisel, gad bar.
Material: Mariposite and serpentine.
Lore: None for mariposite. Serpentine protected its wearers from stinging insects and bites of venomous serpents.
Special attraction: The California Division of Mines and Geology Mineral Museum in Mariposa.
Elevation: 2,700 feet.
Land manager: BLM.
Vehicle type: Any.
For more information: USGS map Coulterville Quadrangle.

SITE 56 *MOTHER LODE MARIPOSITE*

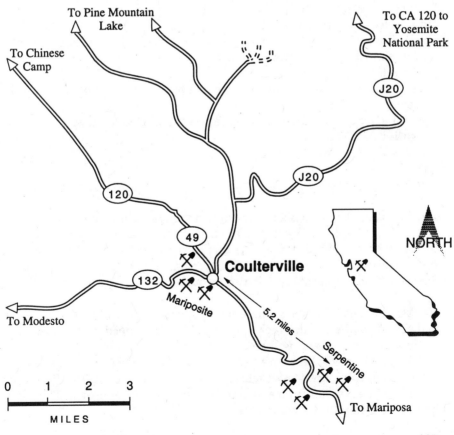

Finding the site: The mariposite site is located in a road cut just west of the junction of California 49 and California 132 at Coulterville and is clearly visible due to its vibrant bluish green coloring.

Rockhounding: Mariposite is a type of mica with a bit of chromium, which colors it a greenish blue color. It is found in white quartz in the Coulterville area. The combination of greenish blue and white is striking. Mariposite makes fine display pieces, but is usually too soft for lapidary work, unless well integrated into the quartz. Serpentine can be found all along CA 49 in road cuts between Mariposa and Coulterville. The quality ranges from poor to good.

The C.D.M.G. Mineral Museum in Mariposa is a highly recommended stop. It is located about 15 miles southwest of Coulterville, in Mariposa, right off of CA 49 at the County Fairground. It has one of the finest gem, mineral, and gold displays in California, as well as mining displays and a children's hands-on mineral collection.

SITE 57 *EUREKA VALLEY SMOKY QUARTZ CRYSTALS*

Land type: Desert hills.
Best season: October to April.
Tools: Rock pick, collecting bag, shovel, gad bar, chisels, crack hammer, gloves, shovel, rake, eye protection.
Material: Smoky quartz crystals.
Lore: Smokey quartz was worn or carried to dispel negative energies, depression, or anger.
Special attractions: Bristlecone Pine forest and Death Valley.
Elevation: 4,500 feet.
Land manager: BLM.
Vehicle type: Any.
For more information: USGS maps Crooked Creek and Chocolate Mountain quadrangles.
Finding the site: From Big Pine head east then northeast on California 168, 13.2 miles. At the junction of CA 168 and White Mountain Road, continue on CA 168 for 12.4 miles more to a dirt road on the left. Take this road 0.3 miles, ignoring the road to the left. Drive another 0.4 miles to a low hill. Seams of smoky quartz crystals run through the hill.

Rockhounding: This site is where smoky quartz crystals are found in seams and pockets in the country rock of the low hill. You'll need gads, chisels, and a crack hammer. Gloves will be useful in protecting your hands. A rake or hand cultivator will be helpful in raking loose crystals from the soil. Be careful in opening crystal pockets so as not to break the crystals. The color of these crystals varies from a light to dark smoky gray or brown. They vary in size from tiny to several inches.

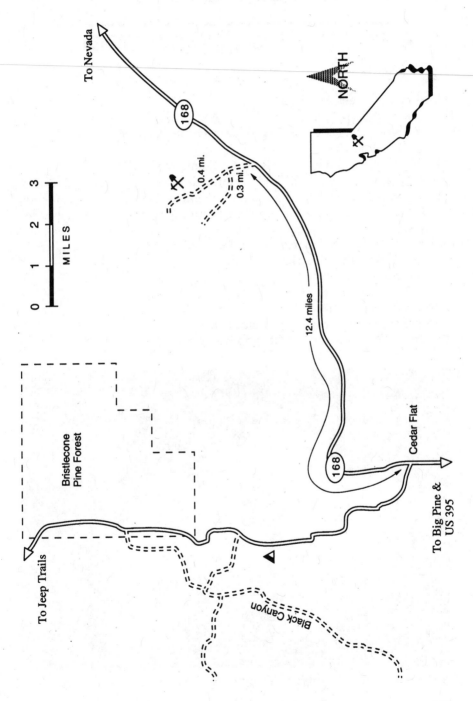

This is a remote site, so if you go here or plan to visit Death Valley National Park, be sure someone knows you're going and take plenty of water.

I've heard that more crystals and some fossils may be found in and around nearby Black Canyon. I have not yet located any there.

SITE 58 *PETERSON MOUNTAIN QUARTZ CRYSTALS*

Land type: Sage-covered hills.
Best season: May to October.
Tools: Rock pick, collecting bag, chisels, shovel, iron rake or hand cultivator.
Material: Clear, milky, rainbow, scepter, amethyst quartz crystals.
Lore: Quartz crystals were and are prized for their healing properties. Amethyst crystals were believed to prevent intoxication (this **is** good news!), bring prophetic dreams, and prevent oversleeping (more good news for today's commuters). Crystals were used in shamanic healing and ritual, and all types were believed to increase and strengthen the aura, the energy field which surrounds the wearer.
Special attraction: None.
Elevation: 4,800 feet.
Land manager: BLM.
Vehicle type: 4X4 or high-clearance truck.
For more information: USGS map Beckworth Quadrangle.

Quartz crystals were thought to have magical and healing qualities by most cultures.

SITE 58 *PETERSON MOUNTAIN QUARTZ CRYSTALS*

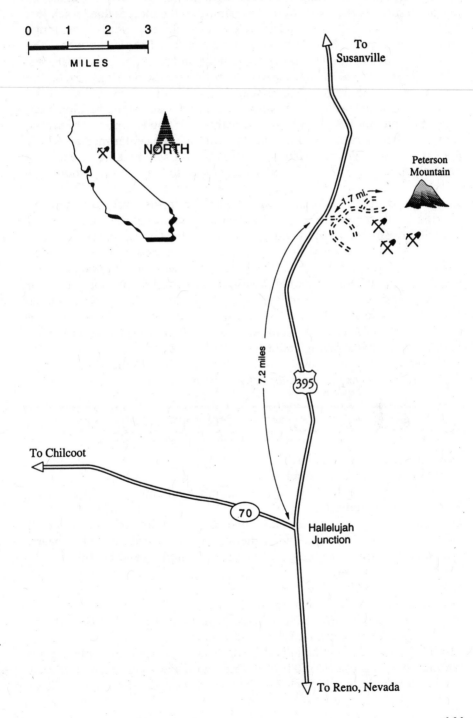

0   1   2   3
MILES

NORTH

To
Susanville

Peterson
Mountain

1.7 mi.

7.2 miles

395

To Chilcoot

70

Hallelujah
Junction

To Reno, Nevada

Finding the site: From the junction of Interstate Highway 395 and California 70, drive north 7.2 miles. Take the dirt road to the right. A barbed-wire gate must be opened then closed after driving through. Drive 1.7 miles, ignoring all roads to the right, always remaining on the most defined road. Just before reaching the site, the road forks. Take the right fork, which is less rough and rutted, although both forks lead to the site. The flat plateau where the road ends provides ample parking and turn-around room for several vehicles.

The crystals are found in seams in the rock near the parking area, on the slopes, and in the dry creek bed near the parking area, as well as on the backside and south side of the mountain that rises above the parking area. Keep in mind that US 395 is a divided highway. If you end up on the wrong side, there are several dirt tracks leading through the center median which are used by the California Highway Patrol. Slow down, making sure that no one is behind you or continue on several miles to a paved turnaround.

Rockhounding: This site has long been known for its lovely and plentiful quartz crystals. There are several digs on the other side of the tall mountain, the tailings piles of which yield up scepter and clear quartz crystals. The easiest way to get around the mountain is to walk around the south side.

Be sure to respect any claim markers, if any. Also, as you walk around the mountain, you will encounter holes near several trees, the tops of which can be seen from the parking area. This is the area where pale lavender amethyst crystals have been dug. If you don't feel up to walking around the mountain, the area around the parking loop will produce many fine specimens. Some are just laying about loose on the ground.

Use your hand cultivator and rake to locate crystals in the dry creek bed or the tailings areas on the other side of the mountain.

SITE 59 *ANTELOPE LAKE ROSE QUARTZ*

Land type: Alpine mountains.
Best season: June to September.
Tools: Rock pick, collecting bag, chisels, crack hammer.
Material: Rose quartz.
Lore: Rose quartz was prized as the stone of love and the healer of emotional pain and trauma. It brought love to the wearer and healed the broken heart.
Special attractions: Antelope Lake fishing, camping, and boating.
Elevation: 7,000 feet.
Land manager: USDAFS.
Vehicle type: Any high-clearance vehicle.
For more information: USDA's Plumas National Forest map or USGS maps Antelope Lake and Babcock Peak quadrangles.
Finding the site: From the junction of 29N43 (road sign states only the last two numbers) and 28N03 (03) near Antelope Lake Dam, head southeast approximately 4 miles to 26N07 (07). On 26N07 head in a southerly direc-

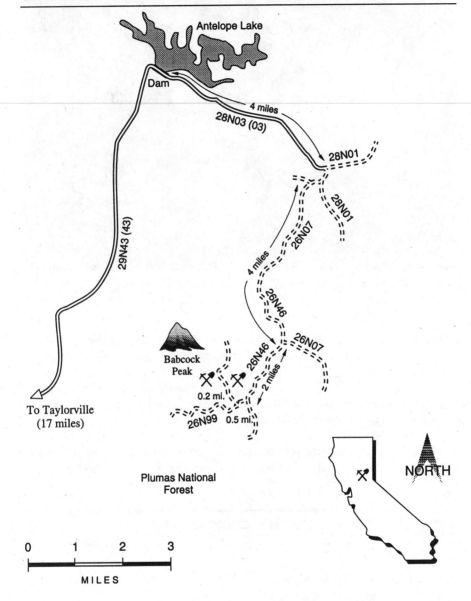

tion for another 4 miles to 26N46 (Forest Service road marker now indicates entire number). Continue southwest approximately 2 miles and make a left on 26N99. On 26N99 drive a half mile and turn north (right) onto an unmarked dirt road with a berm of dirt blocking the center. You may park here and follow the pink float up the low mountain on the right side of the road to several deposits.

Rose quartz—rough, faceted "crystal," tumble-polished and cabochon.

Near the crest of the hill and east is a sizeable deposit of a ruby red quartz. Here I found a piece with a chunk of chrysoprase embedded in it. Although I looked for more, I didn't find any.

To get to the best and highest quality rose quartz deposits, drive around the dirt berm and up the road 0.2 miles. Again follow the rose quartz float to sizeable deposits on both sides of the road.

Rockhounding: This site was once under claim by the Mount Jura Gem and Mineral Society. Although their claim markers still stand, the claims are now open to the public.

SITE 60 *TAYLORVILLE FOSSILS*

Land type: Hills.
Best season: May to September.
Tools: Rock pick, collecting bag.
Material: Fossil shells.
Lore: Worn or carried for longevity. During the Dark Ages it was believed that fossils were those creatures that had failed to be taken aboard Noah's Arc and subsequently died in the Great Flood.
Special attraction: Taylorville Museum.
Elevation: 5,500 feet.
Land manager: USDAFS.

144

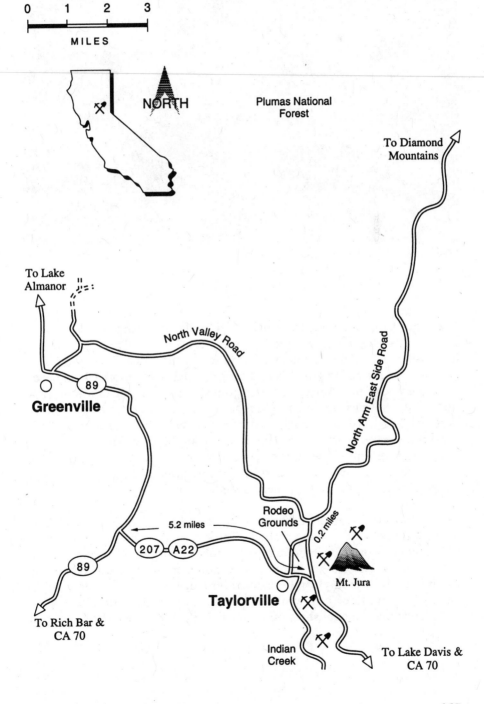

Hunting for fossils at Taylorville.

Vehicle type: Any.

For more information: USGS map Taylorville Quadrangle.

Finding the site: From the junction of California 89 and County Route A22 head west for 5.2 miles to and on through the small town of Taylorville. Turn left just past the rodeo grounds and continue 0.2 miles and park either on the same side of the road as the rodeo grounds or at the base of Mount Jura. Just be sure your car is well off the road. Look for a tall post with the numbers 10 43/22 in yellow paint at waist to shoulder level. The number 15 in brass will be seen farther up. This post marks the area where you take a steep, but short, hike to an area covered with green and red shale. The fossil shells (pectins) occur in the shale as molds and casts. The shells have a well-defined scallop shape of *Glyphaea punctata*.

Rockhounding: This site is easily reached, as Mount Jura, actually a high hill, is right beside the rodeo grounds. There are a few other fossil locations near and on Mount Jura and a couple more along the southeast bank of Indian Creek. These other locations are shown on the accompanying map.

The museum in Taylorville has exhibits of local history and mining. During the Fourth of July weekend the Mount Jura Gem and Mineral Society holds their annual show. Also scheduled for that weekend is a rodeo.

SITE 61 *BUCK'S LAKE SERPENTINE*

Land type: Alpine mountains.
Best season: June to September.
Tools: Rock pick, collecting bag, chisel.
Material: High-quality serpentine.
Lore: Serpentine was worn or carried as a protection against stinging and biting insects and serpents.
Special attractions: Buck's Lake camping, boating, and fishing.
Elevation: 5,700 feet.
Land manager: USDAFS.
Vehicle type: Any.
For more information: USGS map Meadow Valley Quadrangle; USDA's Plumas National Forest map.
Finding the site: From the intersection of Buck's Lake Road and Silver Creek Road, near the town of Meadow Valley, drive southwest for 1.5 miles. On the side of the road for several hundred feet is an outcropping of serpentine. Park safely off to the side at one of the wide spots. Watch carefully for cars coming around the curves, although there is a wide shoulder at the collecting area.

Rockhounding: At this site you will find high-quality chunks of serpentine, with little foliation. The sizes vary from palm-size to watermelon-size.

Although much material is lying on the ground, some collectors may wish to chisel directly from the deposit. Be careful not to let any roll out onto the road. The colors of the serpentine from this site are white, pale green, jade green, and black in varying combinations. This material is suitable for jewelry and other projects.

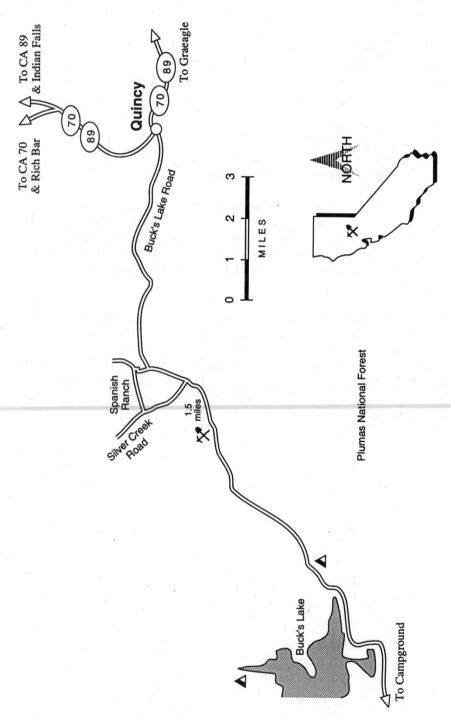

To CA 89
& Indian Falls

To CA 70
& Rich Bar

To Graeagle

Quincy

70

89

70

89

Buck's Lake Road

MILES

0   1   2   3

NORTH

Spanish Ranch

Silver Creek Road

1.5 miles

Plumas National Forest

Buck's Lake

To Campground

SITE 62 *PULGA CALIFORNITE IN SERPENTINE*

Land type: Mountains.
Best season: May to October.
Tools: Rock pick, collecting bag, chisel.
Material: Californite.
Lore: Also known as idocrase, californite was believed to stimulate loyalty and patriotism in its wearer, as well as lessen skin eruptions.
Special attraction: Lake Oroville recreation.
Elevation: 4,500 feet.
Land manager: USDAFS.
Vehicle type: Any.
For more information: USGS map Pulga Quadrangle.
Finding the site: From the intersection of California 70 and Pulga Road, drive 0.9 miles to Camp Creek Road. The road to the site is unpaved and rocky. Low gear on your vehicle will take you up easily. Take Camp Creek Road up 0.7 miles to an outcropping of californite in serpentine on the left, as you are ascending the road. The road to the site has a steep drop-off to your right, so drive carefully. About 100 yards farther up the road is a turnout where you can both turn your vehicle around and park. Low gear is recommended on the way back down to keep brakes from overheating.

Rockhounding: The material at this site has been called both idocrase and vesuvianite, but is actually californite, a compact massive form of idocrase. It has also been nicknamed "California jade." The californite at this location occurs as streaks and lenses in a low-quality serpentine. It is plentiful and is distinguished from the dull and foliated serpentine by its vitreous to pearly luster. The colors of this material are white, light green, dark green, jade green, beige, brown, and black. It is somewhat brittle, but can be used in jewelry and for tumble polishing.

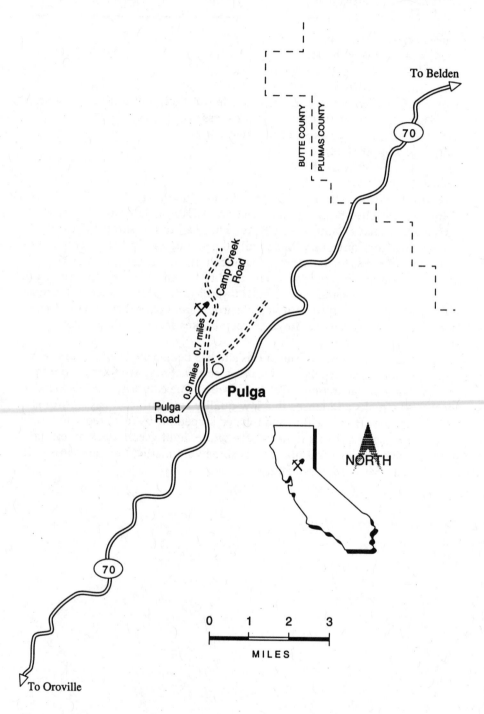

To Belden

BUTTE COUNTY

PLUMAS COUNTY

70

Camp Creek Road

0.7 miles

0.9 miles

Pulga

Pulga Road

NORTH

70

To Oroville

0   1   2   3

MILES

Chiseling californite from a serpentine deposit.

SITE 63 *RICH BAR GOLD*

Land type: Alpine mountains.

Best season: May to October.

Tools: Gold pan, shovel, trowel, rock pick, whisk broom, long-handled screw driver, tweezers, vial, old spoon.

Material: Gold.

Lore: Gold and its ownership meant wealth in historic times much as it does today. Medicinally, gold was used to treat many physical disorders. Today in the United States it is used for the treatment of arthritis.

Special attractions: Nearby fishing, camping, hiking.

Elevation: 3,300 feet.

Land manager: Patented private claim.

Vehicle type: Any.

For more information: Contact Norm or Mike Grant, Rich Bar Mining Co., c/o Pine Air Resort, P.O. Box 39, Twain, CA 95984, or call 916-283-1730.

Finding the site: From the junction of California 70 and California 89 drive west about 4 miles to Twain. It will be on your left. From here drive 8.3 miles to Rich Bar Road. Turn left and follow the road down and across a wooden bridge to the panning booth area.

Rockhounding: This site has been a prolific gold producer since 1850 and is known for the size and purity of the gold nuggets found here. Rich Bar is also the site recounted in a historic book on the area titled *The Shirley*

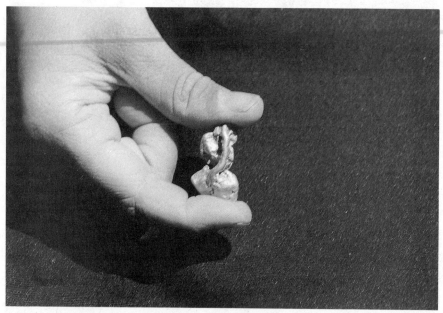

A lucky gold panner found this nugget at Rich Bar.

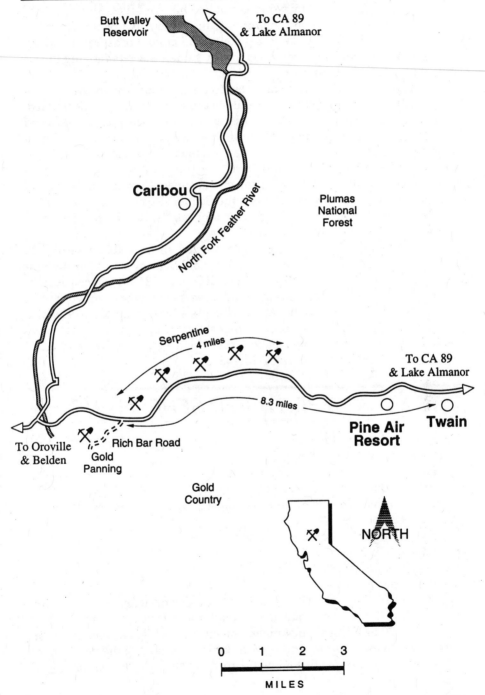

Butt Valley
Reservoir

To CA 89
& Lake Almanor

Caribou

North Fork Feather River

Plumas
National
Forest

Serpentine
4 miles

To CA 89
& Lake Almanor

8.3 miles

**Pine Air
Resort**

Twain

To Oroville
& Belden

Rich Bar Road

Gold
Panning

Gold
Country

NORTH

0   1   2   3

MILES

Letters. This book, written by Louise Clappe, whose pen name was Dame Shirley, gives an interesting, often humorous and sometimes tragic look at what it was like to live and work in a mining camp. It is available at most libraries.

Today the claim is held by Norm Grant and his son Mike. Although they operate a placering plant on the property, they also run a panning concession for those who would like to try their hand at gold prospecting. Many happy gold panners have shown me lovely, golden nuggets ranging in size from a fraction of a pennyweight to several ounces.

For those who don't want to dig their own auriferous (gold-bearing) gravels, a 5 gallon bucket of guaranteed, gold-bearing gravels may be purchased. And these don't contain microscopic pieces, but good-size, plump flakes and small nuggets. Also, Norm Grant will show novices the fine art of gold panning. The Grants have some gold pans on the premises should you forget yours. However, try to bring your own.

This is a fee site. Call or write for current fees. Camping is nearby at Caribou or if one has a yen for luxury, the Grants also own the nearby Pine Air Resort, where you can rent one of many cabins. Reservations are recommended.

If after a visit to Rich Bar, you've contracted an incurable case of gold fever and yearn for information on other gold-bearing areas throughout California, you're in luck. Big Ten Inc., P.O. Box 321231, Cocoa Beach, Florida 32932-1231, publishes maps which show everywhere gold has been found throughout the golden state; and that's a lot of places. Big Ten also publishes maps of gold locations for other states. Your own home state may be one of them! For more information, send them a stamped, self-addressed envelope, or phone them at 1-407-783-4595.

SITE 64 *FEATHER RIVER SERPENTINE*

Land type: Alpine Mountains.
Best season: May to October.
Tools: Rock pick, collecting bag, chisel.
Material: Good grade serpentine.
Lore: Serpentine protects its wearer against stinging insects and the bite of venomous serpents.
Special attraction: Rich Bar gold panning.
Elevation: 3,300 feet.
Land manager: USDAFS.
Vehicle type: Any.
For more information: USGS map Caribou Quadrangle.
Finding the site: From the junction of California 89 and California 70, head west on CA 70 to Twain about 4 miles. You will see the sign to your left. From here drive 4.3 miles. From here to Rich Bar Road, spanning the next 4 miles, will be deposits of serpentine lining the road to your right. Be careful to park

off the road and not allow any serpentine to roll down onto it. Also be watchful of cars and logging trucks coming around corners.

Rockhounding: This site is best visited in conjunction with the Rich Bar site. You can both pan some gold nuggets and collect a good-quality serpentine for lapidary projects.

An item of interest regarding serpentine is that it tends to amass parallel to gold deposits, a valuable bit of lore to keep in mind when searching for that illusive yellow metal!

SITE 65 *WILLARD CREEK AGATE AND JASPER*

Land type: Alpine mountains.
Best season: June to September.
Tools: Rock bag, pick.
Material: Black agate, red jasper, petrified wood.
Lore: Agate and jasper were believed to protect the wearer. Red jasper was favored by archers and also thought to lower fevers. Petrified wood ensured long life.
Special attraction: None.
Elevation: 5,600 feet.
Land manager: BLM.
Vehicle type: Any.
For more information: USGS map Fredonyer Pass Quadrangle.
Finding the site: From Susanville drive 9 miles west to Willard Creek Road. Turn south (left). Willard Creek runs north-south on the east side of the road. The best area to collect is near the creek close to the cattle guard at about 0.3 miles. If you continue down the road another 0.6 miles, the road curves and crosses Willard Creek. Here is another spot to stop and collect.

Rockhounding: This site is best visited early in the season because snow-melt and rain will bring down new material, as it is not overly plentiful here. Willard Creek is a good site to visit in conjunction with the Susanville agate site.

The area where Willard Creek crosses the road is a dandy picnic spot. This site is rumored to have Apache tears, although I didn't find any on my visit.

SITE 65 *WILLARD CREEK AGATE AND JASPER*

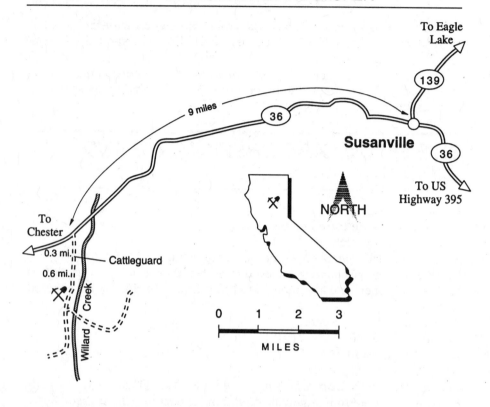

SITE 66 *SUSANVILLE AGATES AND PETRIFIED WOOD*

Land type: Hills.
Best season: May to October.
Tools: Rock pick, collecting bag.
Material: Agate, petrified wood, chalcedony.
Lore: Petrified wood, as was agate, was believed to protect the wearer and lend courage and strength. Petrified wood had the added benefit of insuring its owner a long life. Chalcedony protected its owner against accidents and nightmares.
Special attraction: None.
Elevation: 4,600 feet.
Land manager: BLM.
Vehicle type: Any.
For more information: USGS maps Unison Mountain and Johnstonville quadrangles.

SITE 66 *SUSANVILLE AGATES AND PETRIFIED WOOD*

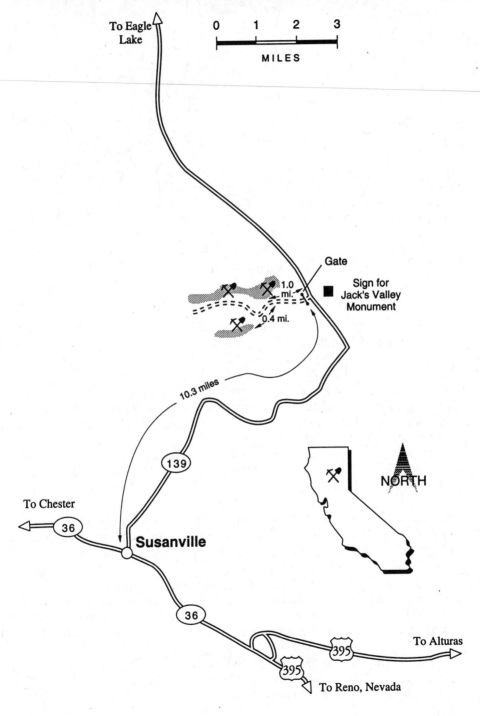

Hunting agate in Dry Creek near Susanville.

Finding the site: From Susanville take California 139 north 10.3 miles to a sign on your right indicating Jack's Valley Monument. Turn west (left) onto a dirt road. To enter the collecting area, you will have to open a gate, drive through, and close the gate. This is cattle country and leaving a gate open is cause for sorrow among the local ranchers. Continue on this dirt road for 1 mile. To the north, about 50 feet from the road, is a dry creek bed. Search along the creek bed and on both sides of the road for agate and petrified wood. Continue 0.4 miles farther where there is a smaller creek bed to the south. At this additional 0.4 miles, both quantity and quality of agate and petrified wood increase throughout the general area. Here also is found some clear to milky chalcedony.

Rockhounding: This site consists of sage-covered, low hills with some large juniper trees. The collecting area is flat on both sides of the road. Although this is cattle country, none were spotted on the day my uncle and I visited this site, although much evidence attested to their presence. The petrified wood found in the dry creek bed is generally light tan with white or cream streaks and makes nice specimen pieces. At the 1.4-mile mark along the road, several palm-size pieces of petrified wood were located in colors of red, cream, brown, gray, and black. These would inspire the lapidary to works of creative jewelry making!

Some of the chalcedony was opalized with white or cream-colored common opal and was found north of the road at the 1.4-mile mark. The agate occurs in mostly red and black.

During summer you may want to confine your collecting to the morning. In August, when I visited, day-time temperatures were running in the 90-degree range.

The collecting material is not abundant, but one half hour of easy walking will garner a bagful of good material. During the month of October, you can also gather handfuls of juniper berries. The dried berries are prized for use in seasoning meats, sauces, and gin!

SITE 67 *CEDARVILLE PETRIFIED WOOD*

Land type: Alpine mountains.
Best season: June to August.
Tools: Rock pick, collecting bag.
Material: Petrified wood, opalite, obsidian.
Lore: Petrified wood was believed to promote long life for its wearer. Opalite, if worn or carried, was thought to foster serenity in accepting one's fate. Black obsidian was used in divination by gazing into its polished surface.
Special attractions: None.
Elevation: 6,600 feet.
Land manager: USDAFS.
Vehicle type: Any.
For more information: USGS maps Cedarville, Warren Peak, and Payne Peak quadrangles.
Finding the site: To get to Site A drive 1.5 miles south on Main Street, heading out of Cedarville toward Gerlach, and take the road to your right just south of the cemetery. Drive this road in a westerly direction for 3.6 miles. On both sides of the road are fair amounts of petrified wood.

To get to Site B from Cedarville take Main Street south, heading toward Gerlach, 3.7 miles to County Road 27 or drive 2.2 miles farther south from Site A. Turn right on County Road 27. At 1.9 miles on the right, on a small rise, will be some opalite, small pieces of gypsum, and chalcedony. At 3 miles slow your car and scan the road edges along the slopes for occasional pieces of petrified wood, especially the areas where runoff or rocks appear to come down off the mountain. At 4.5 miles park your vehicle and walk up the slope to your right. Here the wood is at its most plentiful. The mileages to this site are progressive, so don't reset your mileage indicator.

To reach Site C, head out of Cedarville west from the intersection of Main Street and California 299. Drive 4.9 miles and take the road to your left where a sign indicates skiing. At 0.1 miles follow the road to the left. To continue straight would put you at a locked gate. The road will curve to your left. After an additional 0.1 miles, stop. The right-hand side of the road is littered with coal black obsidian, some of which has a white or gray banding, and occasional pieces of petrified wood.

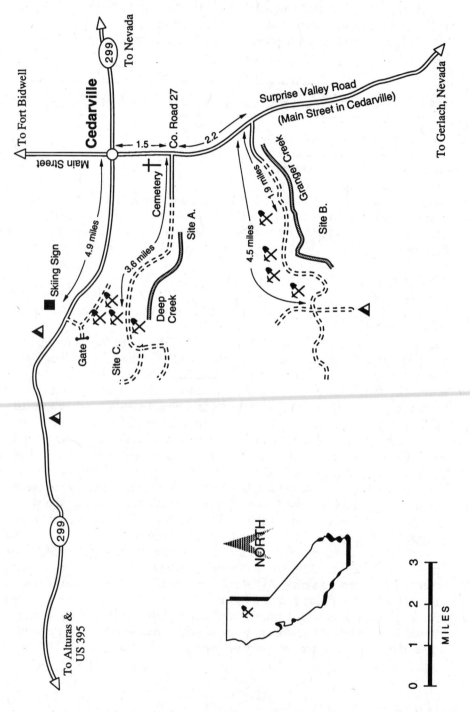

Rockhounding: Dirt roads lead to all of these sites. The petrified wood is of medium to good quality and has been agatized in white, beige, brown, and black, showing excellent wood grain.

The obsidian, though mostly black with gray or white bands, is plentiful and will make nice jewelry. It will whet your appetite for the Davis and Lassen creeks sites.

SITE 68 *DAVIS CREEK OBSIDIAN VARIETIES*

Land type: Alpine mountains.
Best season: June to August.
Tools: Rock pick, collecting bags, gloves, eye protection.
Material: Rainbow, mahogany, black and red obsidian, silver and gray obsidian.
Lore: Rainbow obsidian is thought to bring light, love, and joy to its owner. Mahogany obsidian was worn to help one in attaining physical strength and achieving goals. Red and black obsidian assists one's libido and harmonizes the relations between men and women. Gray or silver and gray obsidian was used in shamanic healing rituals and to assist in astral travel.
Special attraction: None.
Elevation: 7,000 feet.
Land manager: USDAFS.
Vehicle type: Any.
For more information: USGS map Davis Creek Quadrangle.
Finding the site: You must first obtain a permit at Davis Creek Mercantile, in the tiny burg of Davis Creek, in order to collect at any of these sites. The permit is free, but necessary to avoid penalties imposed by the Forest Service. The folks at the Davis Creek Mercantile, Jerry and his wife, Beverly, can provide you with the permit and are helpful with information on the sites. They also have additional maps upon request.

To get to Site A drive north of Davis Creek Mercantile one block on U.S. Highway 395. Turn right and drive 0.8 miles to a triple fork. The left fork goes toward a gate and private land, and the right fork heads to the cemetery. Stay to the center. From this point on, to the right, you will find lots of black obsidian, should you desire to stop and collect.

Site B has the famous rainbow obsidian, as well as a gray and silver variety. Both contain the desired rainbow effects. To get to this site drive 1.5 miles from the triple fork. Ignore the road to the right and drive another 1.2 miles. Take this road to the right and drive another 1.5 miles. Just before the road curves around to the right, you will see a steep track heading up the side of a hill. Just past this there is a spot to your left to pull off and park your car. The small creek here will be a source of refreshment when you return from your hike up the hill. The track up to the site is too steep to drive, and once to the top, there is no place to turn around. Also, the track is littered with sharp shards of obsidian.

SITE 68 *DAVIS CREEK OBSIDIAN VARIETIES*
SITE 69 *LASSEN CREEK RAINBOW AND GREEN-SHEEN*
OBSIDIAN

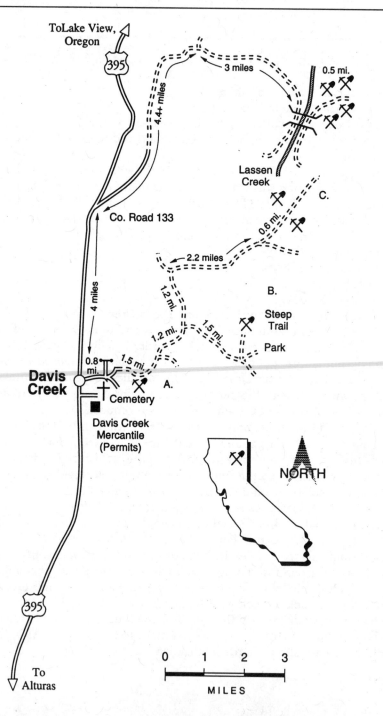

ToLake View, Oregon

395

4.4+ miles

3 miles

0.5 mi.

Lassen Creek

Co. Road 133

C.

0.6 mi.

2.2 miles

1.2 mi.

B.

Steep Trail

4 miles

1.2 mi.

1.5 mi.

Park

0.8 mi.

1.5 mi.

Davis Creek

A.

Cemetery

Davis Creek Mercantile (Permits)

NORTH

395

To Alturas

0   1   2   3

MILES

To get to Site C and the mahogany and red and black obsidian return the 1.5 miles to where you turned off to collect rainbow obsidian and head farther up this main road another 1.2 miles. Ignore the road to the left and continue onward another 2.2 miles, ignoring the road to the right. Another 0.6 miles will bring you to the mahogany and red and black obsidian site. Here the collecting material lines both sides of the road and up the slope to your right, as well as down the slope to your left.

Rockhounding: Site B will require commitment to get to. The climb is steep, and just when you think your going to crest the hill (a very tall hill), you find you're not quite there yet. The climb is only about 0.3 plus miles, but it is steep. The climb is further complicated, near the top, by many sharp pieces of obsidian and pine needles which lay deep under the pine trees. Both make for treacherous walking. The pine needles are slippery, and should you fall, you will be certain to cut yourself on the glass-like obsidian. It would be advisable to wear heavy hiking boots, with contoured soles for maximum traction, heavy denim pants in case you fall, and gloves to protect your hands.

Once up, you will find what looks like black obsidian, some with white or gray banding and another variety that is gray with cream or silver banding. However, look again, some of these pieces will glimmer with iridescent rainbows of light.

You will have to develop "rainbow vision." It took me about a half hour of seemingly fruitless searching before I stumbled upon this technique. Try to search with the sun behind you. Sunlight enhances your ability to see the rainbows. Then look carefully, walking stooped over, scanning the ground. Once I developed my rainbow vision, I began to find one piece after another, fairly consistently. Not all pieces contain rainbows, but many do, and the trip is well worth the hike.

Obsidian is plentiful at this site. The return trip down the steep track can be treacherous also. My technique for returning to my car, laden with several pounds of prime, rainbow obsidian, was to zigzag as I descended. In this way I was able to return without slipping and landing on sharp obsidian.

At Site C you will find lovely pieces of mahogany obsidian, some with black flecks, and black and red obsidian, which is basically a reverse coloration of the mahogany variety. Both are beautiful and make lovely cabochons, belt buckles, and other lapidary creations, as well as great specimens.

Also at this location one will find the unusual obsidian "needles." These are elongated shards of obsidian in various lengths. Davis Creek Mercantile has some almost 1 foot long on display. Most of the needles are only several inches long, but are different and unique and therefore worth collecting while at this site.

Be sure to wear gloves when collecting obsidian. Also wear eye protection if you decide to use your rock pick to chip or break any of it.

One more caution would be to plan your trips to this area not much later than August. This is high elevation and winter comes early and stays late

Rainbow and mahogany obsidian near Davis Creek.

in this part of the country. This is the area where a young couple and their baby were lost when their truck broke down in deep snow, and they attempted to walk out. Eventually they were rescued when the father walked out for help. The area is mostly farm and cattle country and is very sparsely populated. Let someone know when you are going in, how long you'll be, and when you expect to return.

SITE 69 *LASSEN CREEK RAINBOW AND GREEN-SHEEN OBSIDIAN*

Land type: Alpine mountains.
Best season: June to August.
Tools: Rock pick, collecting bag, gloves, eye protection.
Material: Rainbow obsidian, green-sheen obsidian.
Lore: Black obsidian was used by most ancient cultures for divination. Rainbow obsidian, in addition, contained the vibration of joy, while green-sheen obsidian was worn to attract wealth and health.
Special attraction: None.
Elevation: 6,000 feet.
Land manager: USDAFS.
Vehicle type: Any.

United States
Department of
Agriculture

Forest
Service

Modoc NF
Warner Mountain
Ranger District
916-279-6116

Wallace Street
P. O. Box 220
Cedarville, CA 96104
TTY/TDD 916-279-2687

Authorization No. 1994 420

CERTIFICATION OF FREE USE AUTHORIZATION - OBSIDIAN COLLECTION
Warner Mountain Ranger District
Modoc National Forest

THIS PERMIT MUST BE IN YOUR POSSESSION WHEN COLLECTING OR HAULING OBSIDIAN

Permission is granted to the person whose signature is below, to collect obsidian from the lands described on attached map, subject to the conditions listed herein.

The attached map shows the designated collection areas.

In consideration of such permission I agree to:

> Neither sell or exchange any obsidian taken.
> Collect obsidian only in designated areas.
> Use only non-motorized hand tools to excavate.
> Not dig into tree root systems, or cut standing live or dead trees.
> Remove overburden, so as not to dig underground horizontal tunnels.
> Comply with all other regulations governing National Forests.

Maximum annual volume is 500 pounds or approximately six 5 gallon containers.

Final date for removal is: December 31, 1994

Accepted (Signature of permittee)   Date

Nail A. Barber   _8/19/94_

If you wish to be placed on the Warner Mountain Ranger District public information mailing list for future contacts for obsidian collection, leave your name and address with the office receptionist or mail it to: Minerals Officer, Warner Mountain Ranger District, P. O. Box 220, Cedarville, CA 96104.

Caring for the Land and Serving People

FS-6200-28b(3/92)

To collect obsidian get a permit from the Davis Creek store. There is no fee.

For more information: USGS map Sugar Hill Quadrangle.

Finding the site: From Davis Creek head north on U.S. Highway 395 for 4 miles. Turn right on County 133 and drive in a northerly direction for 4.4 miles. Turn right and drive 3 miles to the bridge. Cross the bridge and turn left. Drive a half mile to the obsidian site.

Rockhounding: At 0.5 miles you will see numerous shallow pits on both sides of the road. Obsidian will be scattered all over. The material is abundant here. From a distance all the obsidian at this site appears to be plain black. Closer inspection reveals both rainbow and green-sheen obsidian. Keeping the sun to your back you can locate both types. The rainbow obsidian is more plentiful than the sheen, but you need only look a short time in order to find several pieces of the sheen.

It is helpful to use your rock pick to chip the edges of the obsidian in order to reveal a fresh surface, in some cases. Be sure to wear eye protection when doing this. Obsidian fragments can be nearly invisible and very sharp. This is the site where I got a sliver of obsidian in my finger because I was not wearing my gloves as I should have been.

There is also supposed to be gold-sheen, blue-sheen, and silver-sheen obsidian at this sight. I did not find any of those on my trip in the summer of 1994.

SITE 70 *SHASTA AREA COPPER MINERALS*

Land type: Hills.

Best season: May to September.

Tools: Rock pick, collecting bag.

Material: Chalcocite, chalcopyrite, malachite, chrysocolla.

Lore: No lore available on chalcocite or chalcopyrite. Malachite, worn or carried, was believed to assist one during times of change or disruption. It was also thought to facilitate an understanding of the mind/body link in illness. Chrysocolla was worn for its calming and energizing properties.

Special attractions: Mount Shasta scenic vistas and camping; Shasta Lake limestone caverns.

Elevation: 4,100 feet.

Land manager: USDAFS.

Vehicle type: Any.

For more information: USGS maps Juniper Flat and The Whaleback quadrangles.

Finding the site: The road to this site is located 0.3 plus miles southwest of the junction of California 97 and County Route A12. Turn north onto Yellow Butte Road and continue 1 mile. Turn onto the road to your left and drive 0.1 miles.

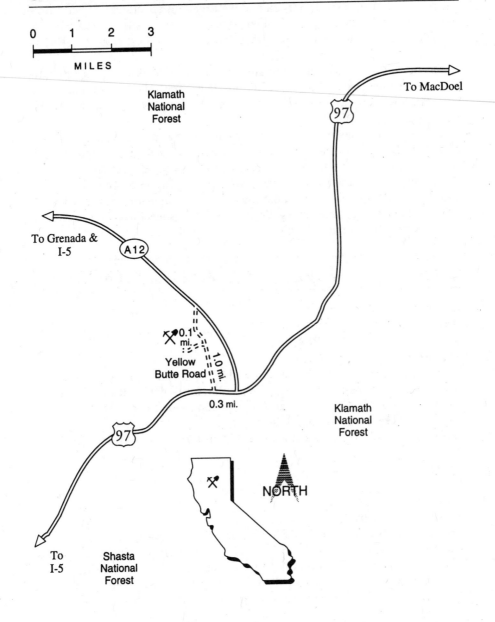

0   1   2   3

MILES

Klamath
National
Forest

To MacDoel

97

To Grenada &
I-5

A12

⚒0.1
mi.

Yellow
Butte Road

1.0 mi.

0.3 mi.

Klamath
National
Forest

97

NORTH

To
I-5

Shasta
National
Forest

Mt. Shasta

Rockhounding: Dark gray chalcocite, metallic chalcopyrite, green malachite, and bluish green chrysocolla are found on the dumps of an old copper mine. All four copper minerals make excellent specimens for addition to a mineral collection. Rarely, lapidary-grade malachite and chrysocolla can be collected as well, although the pieces are small. For best results, use your rock pick to dig into the tailings.

Mount Shasta, south on Interstate 5 from the collecting site, is a beautiful area. Around the small town of Mt. Shasta are several campgrounds. Book stores in town have a wide variety of books on Mount Shasta's mystical history.

The mountain has been the site of many strange and unusual sightings of ancient Lemurians and UFOs. Native Americans have many legends concerning the mystical nature of this area. There are several campgrounds here.

Farther south down I-5 is Shasta Lake. Camping and boating may be enjoyed here. The feature of most interest is the limestone caverns where visitors can see large limestone galleries filled with stalactites and stalagmites of interesting proportions. Guided tours are available.

SITE 71 *EEL RIVER JADE AND CROCIDOLITE*

Land type: Oak-covered hills.
Best season: May to October.
Tools: Rock pick, collecting bag.
Material: Jade, crocidolite.
Lore: Jade, worn or carried, was believed to bring wealth, luck and wisdom. According to New Age lore, crocidolite, a blue form of asbestos or riebeckite, enhances one's mathematical abilities. (Good news for recalcitrant check balancers.) On a less mundane level it heightens intuition and aids one in separating media hype and salesmanship from the truly important things in life.
Special attraction: None.
Elevation: 3,000 feet.
Land manager: BLM.
Vehicle type: Any.
For more information: USGS map Mina Quadrangle.
Finding the site: From Covelo drive 12.4 miles north on California 162 to the junction of Bald Mountain Road. From here continue on CA 162 another 4.7 miles to the bridge crossing the north fork of the Eel River. Check along the riverbed for jade in shades from white to dark green and crocidolite.

Rockhounding: The collectibles here are the jade and crocidolite. There is also some purplish chert which could be considered "leaverite" material.

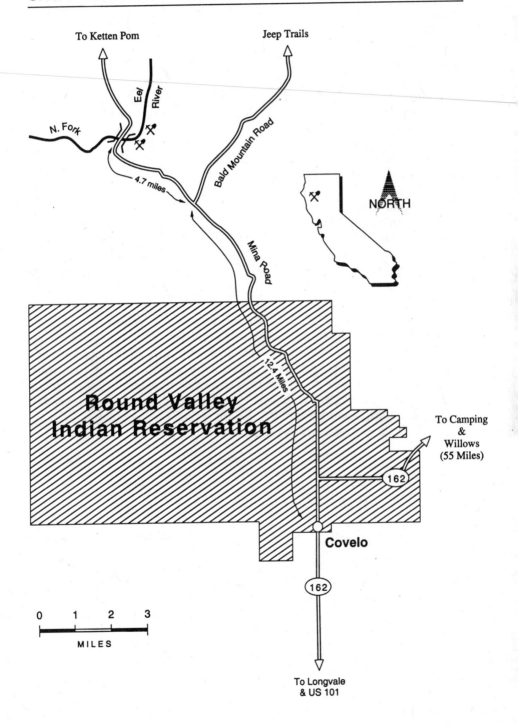

SITE 72 *COLORFUL JASPER AND JADE NEAR COVELO*

Land type: Oak-covered hills.
Best season: May to September.
Tools: Rock pick, collecting bag.
Material: Jasper and jade.
Lore: Jasper was worn for protection in battle and to promote courage. North American Indians used it in rain-bringing rituals. Jade attracted wealth, luck, love, and wisdom.
Special attraction: None.
Elevation: 3,000 feet.
Land manager: USDAFS.
Vehicle type: Any.
For more information: USGS map Newhouse Ridge Quadrangle.
Finding the site: In the town of Covelo take California 162 heading north. It will swing east. Continue 10.5 miles to the bridge crossing the Middle Fork of the Eel River. The area to the west of the bridge is the best area to collect.

Rockhounding: The jasper at this site comes in red, yellow, brown, and rusty red. White patterning makes this material desirable for lapidary projects. Jade can also be found in this area, but takes a bit more looking. Much of the jade that is found is of poor quality. However, if you plan your trip for early in the season, winter rain and snow-melt coming down from the mountains will restore both jasper and jade quantities. The jade comes in several shades, ranging from light to dark green or a combination of these colors, with some pieces occurring in white.

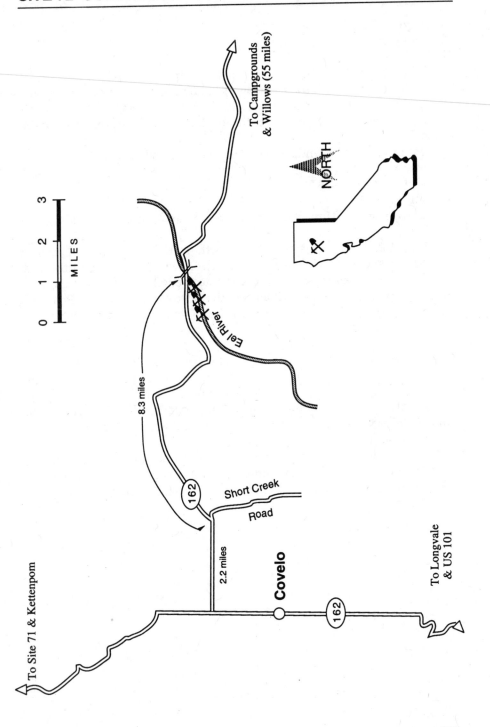

SITE 73 *HEARST COLLECTIBLES*

Land type: Hills.
Best season: April to October.
Tools: Rock pick, collecting bag.
Material: Banded rhyolite, jade, actinolite, jasper.
Lore: Rhyolite was used by the ancients in balms for curing circulatory and skin problems. Jade promotes wealth, luck, love, and wisdom. Actinolite has similar, although milder, properties to jade, but also aids in promoting brotherhood.
Special attraction: Mendocino County Museum in Willits.
Elevation: 2,200 feet.
Land manager: USDAFS.
Vehicle type: Any.
For more information: USGS maps Willits and Foster Mountain quadrangles.
Finding the site: From Willits head north on U.S. Highway 101 a short distance to Reynolds Highway. Turn right. Drive 12.8 miles on this road, which becomes Hearst-Willits Road. Stay to the left. If you turn right onto it, you will wind up back in Willits near the airport. Hearst-Willits Road will take you to the bridge that crosses the Eel River. Park and search up and down the river area.

Rockhounding: This site is another that is best visited early in the season, after spring runoff renews the availability of collecting material. This is the time when larger pieces of jade will more likely be found.

Banded rhyolite, actinolite in green hues, jade in white and green, and colorful jasper in warm red, orange, yellow, and white are the collectibles of interest here.

The Mendocino County Museum offers visitors a look at the history of Mendocino County from early Indian cultures to the present day. There is also a botanical garden containing indigenous plant species.

SITE 73 *HEARST COLLECTIBLES*

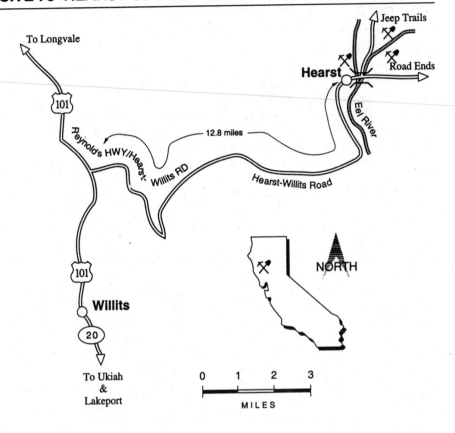

To Longvale

Jeep Trails

Hearst

Road Ends

Eel River

101

12.8 miles

Reynold's HWY/Hearst-Willits RD

Hearst-Willits Road

101

Willits

20

To Ukiah
&
Lakeport

NORTH

0   1   2   3

MILES

SITE 74 *BLACK BUTTE RESERVOIR SHOWY JASPER*

Land type: Hills.
Best season: April to November.
Tools: Rock pick, collecting bag.
Material: Jasper, agate, petrified wood.
Lore: Jasper and agate were worn for protection and courage. Red jasper was prized by archers, while green was inscribed with a magic symbol and worn for digestive problems. Jasper was an important ingredient in American Indian rain-bringing rituals. Petrified wood was believed to bestow its wearer with long life.
Special attractions: Black Butte Reservoir boating and camping.
Elevation: 3,400 feet.
Land manager: BLM.
Vehicle type: Any.
For more information: USGS maps Chrome, Julian Rocks, Sehorn Creek, and Black Butte Dam quadrangles.
Finding the site: From the town of Elk Creek take the Lagoda-Stoneyford Road north a half mile. From the junction of this road, which runs along Stoney Creek and California 162, you can collect some jasper if you continue east along Stoney Creek for 3.5 miles. At the 3.5-mile mark you will encounter CA 162 coming in from the west. Continue north another mile. You will see a road to the right, which heads in a easterly direction. Jasper can be collected along this road that follows Stoney Creek in an east-northeast direction.

For more jasper, some agate, and petrified wood, continue again north on Lagoda-Stoneyford Road about 8.5 miles to Newville Road. Turn right and head for Black Butte Reservoir, another 7 miles. All along the shores of the reservoir you can find jasper, agate, and petrified wood.

Rockhounding: Good collecting can be had near the Buckhorn Campground and the head of Burris Creek at the east side of the reservoir. You may discover, as I did, that some of your jasper samples have inclusions of marcasite. Most of the jasper and agate come in red, orange, yellow, and green.

When the water level in the reservoir drops at summer's end and into the fall, more material can be found along the shoreline.

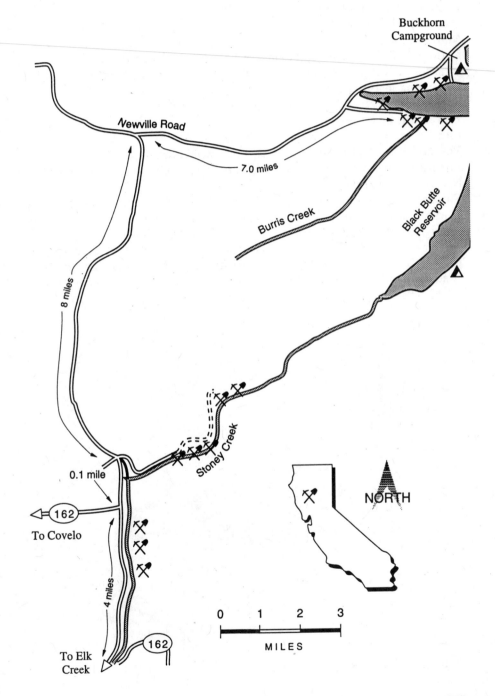

Buckhorn
Campground

Newville Road

7.0 miles

Burris Creek

Black Butte
Reservoir

8 miles

Stoney Creek

0.1 mile

162

To Covelo

4 miles

162

To Elk
Creek

NORTH

0   1   2   3
MILES

175

SITE 75 *GOAT MOUNTAIN MOSS AGATE*

Land type: Alpine mountains.
Best season: June to September.
Tools: Rock pick, collecting bag.
Material: Moss agate.
Lore: This stone was thought to insure a green thumb to one wishing to plant a garden. It was also believed to heal the pain of a stiff neck and to assist in locating lost treasure.
Special attraction: Letts Lake recreation.
Elevation: 6,000 feet.
Land manager: USDAFS.
Vehicle type: 4X4 or high clearance two-wheel-drive.
For more information: USGS map Fouts Spring Quadrangle; Mendocino National Forest map.
Finding the site: From Interstate 5 exit at the Maxwell offramp in the town of Maxwell and drive west through town. Remain on this road. You will pass through the town of Logoda to the town of Stoneyford. Turn left at the Forest Service work station and continue on Fouts Spring Road (M10). Stay on M10 to Dixie Glade, turn left, and head toward Letts Lake. Pass the lake and continue 3 miles to the Board Springs housing tract. At the first two-way turn go left and continue 0.2 plus miles. Take the road to the left, which will go

Goat Mountain moss agate. Polished and rough.

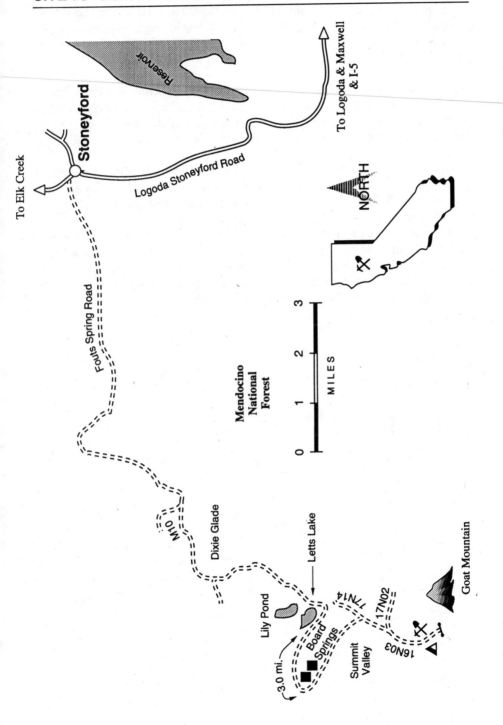

up the hill to a log landing. Turn right. Turn left on Second Way and drive through the housing tract. Second Way becomes Crossing Road. Follow this road toward Summit Valley. Take 17N14 to 17N02 to 16N03. You should see a sign indicating Goat Mountain Lookout. On your right will be a small, unimproved campground just before you reach a gate. The moss agate is located across from the camp on the sides of a bare mountain.

Rockhounding: This site comes courtesy of Herman Schob, a friend of mine and occasional partner in rockhounding. It is located approximately 50 miles from the town of Maxwell. One must drive mostly dirt roads, some regularly maintained and some not, from the town of Stoneyford to the collecting site.

The moss agate is translucent to snow white, with plentiful black inclusions of moss-like dendrites and containing occasional small pockets of drusy quartz crystals. Some of the material has mustard yellow speckling. It makes fabulous cabochons and is great for tumbling.

Although not a day trip, this site would be great for a weekend or weeklong trip. A historic marker at Letts Lake marks this as the site of an old gold claim. There are fishing and camping available at Letts Lake.

Pack a picnic lunch to this site. Herman says the view from here to the Sacramento Valley and yonder buttes is spectacular!

APPENDIX A: *SOURCES USED FOR THIS GUIDE*

Geology Underfoot in Southern California, by Robert P. Sharp and Allen F. Glazner, Mountain Press, Missoula, Montana: 1993

Fossils in America, by Jay Ellis Ransom, Harper & Row Publishers, New York, New York: 1964

Simon & Schuster's Guide to Rocks and Minerals, edited by Martin Prinz, George Harlow, and Joseph Peters, Simon & Schuster, New York, New York: 1977

The Audubon Society Field Guide to North American Rocks and Minerals, by Charles W. Chesterman, Alfred A. Knopf, Inc., New York, New York: 1978

Minerals of the World, by Charles A. Sorrell, Western Publishing Co., Racine, Wisconsin: 1973

The Earth, an Introduction to Physical Geology, by Edward J. Tarbuck and Frederick K. Lutgens, Charles E. Merrill Publishing Co., Columbus, Ohio: 1984

Crystal, Gem & Metal Magic, by Scott Cunningham, Llewellyn Publications, St. Paul, Minnesota: 1991

Love is in the Earth - A Kaleidoscope of Crystals, by Melody, Earth-Love Publishing House, Wheatridge, Colorado: 1991

APPENDIX B: *FURTHER READING AND INFORMATION*

The Week-end Rock Hound, by A.H. Ryan, Gem Guide Books Co., Pico Rivera, California: 1970

Ultraviolet Guide to Minerals, by Sterling Gleason, D. Van Nostrand Co. Ltd., Toronto, Canada: 1960

Prospecting for Gemstones and Minerals, by John Sinkankas, Van Nostrand Reinhold Co. New York, New York: 1961

Big Ten's Gold Maps of California, by Charles Overbey, Cocoa Beach, Florida

Healing With Crystals and Gemstones, by Daya Sarai Chocron, Samuel Weiser, Inc., York Beach, Maine: 1986

Everybody Needs a Rock, by Byrd Baylor, Macmillan Publishing Co., New York, New York: 1974

Rock & Gem magazine, Ventura, California

Lapidary Journal, Devon, Pennsylvania

Jewelry Crafts magazine, Ventura, California

APPENDIX C: ROCKHOUND CLUBS AND ORGANIZATIONS

Rock and mineral clubs provide rockhounds with a variety of services, such as the companionship of like-minded people. They offer weekend fieldtrips, an annual show where members can display and sell their jewelry or special finds, and interesting programs and workshops. Many extend training in lapidary and silversmithing skills. Some clubs have their own claims, which are open to collection for members, or the members may have knowledge of collecting sites that are not widely known. Rockhounds can greatly widen their horizons by joining a rockhounding group.

ROCKHOUND ORGANIZATIONS

Amador County Gem & Mineral Society
5 Broad St.
Sutter Creek, CA 95685

American Opal Society
P.O. Box 382
Anaheim, CA 92815

American River Gem & Min. Soc.
P.O. Box 1376
Fair Oaks, CA 95661

Antelope Valley Gem & Min. Club
P.O. Box 69
Lancaster, CA 93584

Antiock Lapidary Club
P.O. Box 91
Antioch, CA 94509

Autonetics Gem & Min. Club
5425 Vista Linda
Yorba Linda, CA 92687

Bear Gulch Rock Club
P.O. Box 304
Ontario, CA 91764

Berkeley Gem & Min. Soc.
P.O. Box 755
Berkeley, CA 94701

Boulder Buster Geology Study Group
245 E. Thomson Ave.
Sonoma, CA 95476

Cal City-Edwards Gem & Min. Club
P.O. Box 2307
California City, CA 93504

Calaveras Gem & Mineral Society
P.O. Box 517
Angeles Camp, CA 95222

Campbell Gem & Mineral Club
P.O. Box 217
Campbell, CA 95009-0217

Capistrano Valley Rock & Min. Club
P.O. Box 279
San Clemente, CA 92674

Carmel Valley Gem & Min. Soc.
P.O. Box 5846
Carmel, CA 93921

Carmichael Gem & Mineral Society
2040 Waterford Rd.
Sacramento, CA 95815

Centinela Valley Gem & Min. Club
5316 W. 82nd St.
Los Angeles, CA 90045

Coalinga Rockhounds Society
P.O. Box 652
Coalinga, CA 93210

Conejo Gem & Mineral Club
P.O. Box 723
Newbury Park, CA 91319

Contra Costa Mineral & Gem Society
P.O. Box 4667
Walnut Creek, CA 94596

Culver City Rock & Min. Club
P.O. Box 3324
Culver City, CA 90231

Davis-Woodland Gem & Mineral Society
630 E. St.
Davis, CA 95616

Del-Air Rockhounds Club
P.O. Box 7618
Van Nuys, CA 91409

Delvers Gem & Mineral Society
Box 4115
Downey, CA 90241

East Bay Mineral Society
2506 High St.
Oakland, CA 94601

Eastern Sierra Rock & Min. Soc.
P.O. Box 1156
Mammoth Lakes, CA 93546

El Cajon Valley Gem & Min. Soc.
P.O. Box 451
El Cajon, CA 92022

El Dorado County Min. & Gem Soc.
P.O.Box 950
Placerville, CA 95667

Estero Bay Gem & Min. Soc.
P.O. Box 248
Morro Bay CA 93443

Faceters Guild of Nor. Calif.
4270 Silver Crest Ave.
Sacramento, CA 95821

Faceters Guild of So. Calif.
P.O. Box 8890-436
Fountain Valley, CA 92708

Fairfield Lapidary Society
P.O. Box 603
Fairfield, CA 94533

Fallbrook Gem & Min. Soc.
P.O. Box 62
Fallbrook, CA 92028

Foothill Gem & Mineral Society
6265 Altura Ave.
La Crescenta, CA 91214

Forester Rockhounds #779
4680 Mt. Armet Dr.
San Diego, CA 92117

Fossils for Fun Society
1449 Sebastian Way
Sacramento, CA 95864

Fresno Gem & Min. Soc.
340 W. Olive
Fresno, CA 93728

Galileo Gem Guild
199 Museum Way
S. San Francisco, CA 94080

Gem Carvers Guild
230 Churchill Glen
Sierra Madre, CA 91024

Gemological Society of San Diego
P.O. Box 1448
Spring Valley, CA 91979

Glendale Verdugo Gem & Min. Soc.
P.O. Box 265
Montrose, CA 91021

Glendora Gems
859 E. Sierra Ave.
Glendora, CA 91740

Golden Empire Mineral Soc.
P.O. Box 1212
Chico, CA 95927

Hollister Gem & Lapidary Club
P.O. Box 438
Hollister, CA 95024

Hollywood Lapidary & Min. Soc.
2529 W. Temple St.
Los Angeles, CA 90026

Humboldt Gem & Mineral Society
P.O. Box 1075
Eureka, CA 95501

Imperial Valley Gem & Min. Soc.
P.O. Box 1721
El Centro, CA 92244

Indian Wells Gem & Mineral Society
P.O. Box 1481
China Lake, CA 93555

Islanders Gem & Mineral Soc.
P.O. Box 21007
El Cajon, CA 92021

Kaiser Rock & Gem Club
15380 Orchid St.
Fontana, CA 92325

Kern County Mineral Society
11800 Brockridge Ct.
Bakersfield, CA 93305

Kings Stonecrafters
1325 Beulah St.
Hanford, CA 93238

La Puente Gem & Mineral Club
P.O. Box 647
La Puente, CA 91744

Lake County Diamond & Min. Soc.
P.O. Box 272
Nice, CA 95464

Lake Elsinore Gem & Min. Soc.
33040 Dowman
Lake Elsinore, CA 92530

Lassen Gem & Mineral Society
P.O. Box 161
Susanville, CA 96130

Livermore Valley Lithophiles
P.O. Box 626
Livermore, CA 94550

Lodi Gem & Mineral Society
P.O. Box 572
Lodi, CA 95241

Long Beach Mineral & Gem Soc.
P.O. Box 4082
Long Beach, CA 90804

Los Angeles Lapidary Society
2517 Federal Ave.
Los Angeles, CA 90064

Los Angeles Mineralogical Soc.
228 S. Oxford Ave.
Los Angeles, CA 90004

Marin Mineral Society
P.O. Box 150345
San Rafael, CA 94915-0345

Mariposa Gem & Mineral Club
P.O. Box 753
Mariposa, CA 95338

Mendocino Coast Gem & Min. Soc.
P.O. Box 868
Fort Bragg, CA 95437

Merced Gem & Mineral Society
P.O. Box 607
Merced, CA 95340

Mineral & Gem Soc. of Castro Valley
P.O. Box 2145
Castro Valley, CA 94546

Min. Research Soc. of So. Calif.
4759 Blackthorne Ave.
Long Beach, CA 90808

Mineralogical Soc. of So. Calif.
P.O. Box 41027
Pasadena, CA 91104

Modoc Gem & Mineral Society
P.O. Box 465
Alturas, CA 96101

Mojave Desert Gem & Mineral Soc.
25647 W. Main
Barstow, CA 92311

Monrovia Rockhounds
P.O. Box 553
Monrovia, CA 91016

Mother Lode Mineral Society
P.O. Box 1263
Modesto, CA 95353

Mt. Jura Gem & Mineral Society
P.O. Box 194
Taylorville, CA 95983

Needles Gem & Mineral Club
P.O. Box 762
Needles, CA 92363

North Island Gem & Min. Society
P.O. Box 20772
El Cajon, CA 92021

No. Calif. Mineralogical Assn.
P.O. Box 27
Point Arena, CA 95468

Orange Belt Mineralogical Soc.
P.O. Box 5642
San Bernardino, CA 92412

Orange County 49ers
P.O. Box 781
Midway City, CA 92655

Oxnard Gem & Mineral Society
P.O. Box 246
Oxnard, CA 93032

Palmdale Gem & Mineral Society
P.O. Box 900279
Palmdale, CA 93590

Palos Verdes Gem & Min. Society
P.O. Box 686
Lomita, CA 90717

Pasadena Lapidary Society
P.O. Box 5025
Pasadena, CA 91117

Mojave Mineralogical Society
P.O. Box 511
Boron, CA 93596

Monterey Bay Mineral Society
P.O. Box 12
Salinas, CA 93901

Mother Lode Mineralites
P.O. Box 9498
Auburn, CA 95604

Napa Valley Rock & Gem Society
P.O. Box 404
Napa, CA 94559

Nevada County Gem & Min. Soc.
P.O. Box 565
Nevada City, CA 95959

North Orange County Gem & Min. Soc.
P.O. Box 653
La Habra, CA 90633

Northrop Recreation Gem & Min Club
1 Northrop Ave.
Hawthorne, CA 90025

Orange Coast Min. & Lapidary Soc.
P.O. Box 10175
Costa Mesa, CA 92626

Orcutt Mineral Society
P.O. Box 106
Santa Maria, CA 93454

Pajaro Valley Rockhounds
361 Manor Ave.
Watsonville, CA 95076

Palomar Gem & Mineral Club
P.O. Box 1583
Escondido, CA 92033

Paradise Gem & Mineral Club
P.O. Box 692
Paradise, CA 95967

Peninsula Gem & Geology Soc.
P.O. Box 952
Los Altos, CA 94022

Pomona Rockhounds
P.O. Box 194
Pomona, CA 91769

Ramona Advenure & Treasure Seekers
P.O. Box 597
Hemet, CA 92546-0597

Rancho Santa Margarita
Gem & Min. Soc.
P.O. Box 355
San Luis Rey, CA 92068

Redwood Gem & Mineral Society
P.O. Box 203
Santa Rosa, CA 95402

Rockatomics Gem & Min. Soc.
P.O. Box 346
Canoga Park, CA 91307

Roseville Rock Rollers
P.O. Box 212
Roseville, CA 95678

Sacramento Valley Detecting Buffs
4910 Ortega St.
Sacramento, CA 95820

San Diego Mineral & Gem Society
Spanish Village, Balboa Park
San Diego, CA 92101

San Fernando Valley Min. & Gem Soc.
P.O. Box 21
N. Hollywood, CA 91603

San Gorgonio Mineral & Gem Soc.
P.O. Box 424
Banning, CA 92220

San Pablo Bay Gem & Min. Soc.
P.O. Box 636
San Pablo, CA 94806

Santa Barbara Min. & Gem Soc.
P.O. Box 815
Santa Barbara, CA 93102

Santa Cruz Mineral & Gem Soc.
P.O. Box 343
Santa Cruz, CA 95061

Porterville Area Gem
& Min. Soc.
10 Olive Dr.
Porterville, CA 93257

Rancho Bernardo Rockhounds
16955 Bernardo Oaks Dr.
San Diego, CA 92128

Red Bluff Lapidarists
P.O. Box 435
Red Bluff, CA 96080

Riverside Treasure Hunters
16454 Washington Dr.
Fontana, CA 92335

Rockcrafters Club
2540 Orange Ave.
La Crescenta, CA 91214

Sacramento Mineral Society
P.O. Box 160544
Sacramento, CA 95816

San Diego Lapidary Society
5641 Mildred St.
San Diego, CA 92110

San Dieguito Gem & Min. Soc.
P.O. Box 863
Encinitas, CA 92024

San Francisco Gem & Min. Soc.
4234 Judah St.
San Francisco, CA 94122

San Luis Obispo Gem & Min. Club
P.O. Box 563
San Luis, CA 93406

Santa Ana Rock & Mineral Club
P.O. Box 51
Santa Ana, CA 92702

Santa Clara Valley Gem & Min. Soc.
P.O. Box 54
San Jose, CA 95103

Santa Lucia Rockhounds
P.O. Box 1672
Paso Robles, CA 93447

Santa Monica Gemological Soc.
P.O. Box 652
Santa Monica, CA 90404

Searcher Gem & Mineral Society
Box 3492
Anaheim, CA 92803

Sequoia Gem & Mineral Society
P.O. Box 1245
Redwood City, CA 94064

Shadow Mountain Gem & Min. Soc.
P.O. Box 358
Cathedral City, CA 92234

Sierra Pelona Rock Club
P.O. Box 699
Newhall, CA 91321

South Lake Tahoe Gem & Min. Soc.
P.O. Box 7186
S. Lake Tahoe, CA 96158

So. Calif. Paleontological Soc.
1826 9th St.
Manhattan Beach, CA 90266

Stockton Lapidary & Min. Soc.
3136 E. Anita
Stockton, CA 95205

Sutter Buttes Gem & Min. Soc.
P.O. Box 268
Marysville, CA 95901

Tourmaline Gem & Mineral Soc.
La Mesa, CA 92041

Tule Gem & Mineral Society
P.O. Box 1061
Visalia, CA 93279

Vallejo Gem & Mineral Society
P.O. Box 389
Vallejo, CA 94589

Valley of the Moon Gem & Min. Club
P.O. Box 583
Sonoma, CA 95476

Santa Rosa Mineral & Gem Soc.
P.O. Box 7036
Santa Rosa, CA 95407

Searles Lake Gem & Min. Soc.
P.O. Box 966
Trona, CA 93562

Sequoia Mineral Society
4954 N. Del Mar
Fresno, CA 93704

Shasta Gem & Mineral Society
P.O. Box 424
Redding, CA 96099

South Bay Lapidary & Min. Soc.
P.O. Box 1606
Torrance, CA 90505

So. Calif. Micromineralogists
4759 Blackthorne Ave.
Long Beach, CA 90808

Southwest Rockwranglers
1824 W. Rosecrans
Gardena, CA 90249

Superior Calif. Gem & Min. Assn.
P.O. Box 144
Chico, CA 95927

Tehachapi Valley Gem & Min. Soc.
P.O. Box 4400-132
Tehachapi, CA 93561

Trinity Gem & Mineral Society
P.O. Box 159
Weaverville, CA 96093

Vava Valley Gem & Min. Soc.
P.O. Box 368
Vacaville, CA 95696

Valley Gems
9050 1/2 West Avenue J
Lancaster, CA 93536

Valley Prospectors
P.O. Box 2923
San Bernardino, CA 92406

Ventura Gem & Mineral Society
P.O. Box 1573
Ventura, CA 93002

Victor Valley Gem & Min. Club
15056 B 7th St.
Victorville, CA 92307

VIP Gem & Mineral Society
7357 Hesperia Ave.
Reseda, CA 91335

Vista Gem & Mineral Society
P.O. Box 1641
Vista, CA 92083

W.L.A. Japanese American League
1928 Armacost Ave.
Los Angeles, CA 90025

West End Prospectors
P.O. Box 834
Fontana, CA 92335

Westside Mineralogists
1826 9th St.
Manhattan Beach, CA 90266

Whittier Gem & Mineral Society
P.O. Box 66
Whittier, CA 90608

Willits Gem & Mineral Club
4500 Canyon Rd.
Willits, CA 95490

Woodland Hills Rock Chippers
P.O. Box 205
Woodland, Hills, CA 91365

Yucaipa Valley Gem & Min. Soc.
P.O. Box 494
Yucaipa, CA 92399

Joining a rockhound club allows one to enjoy the fun of mineral collecting with like-minded individuals.

ABOUT THE AUTHOR

Gail A. Butler was born in California, as were her parents. This in itself is noteworthy, since there are not many people that were actually born in California, most having imported themselves.

Gail has been a rockhound all her life and continually works to improve her lapidary skills, as well as discover new areas to collect rocks and minerals. She is also an avid and successful gold prospector who spends many weekends panning and sluicing cold, mountain streams or metal detecting dry, mountain washes, for that illusive golden metal for which California is so well known. Gold!

An avid explorer and accomplished wilderness camper, she has spent much time prospecting for rocks, minerals, gold, and lost treasure in the deserts and mountains of California.

Many of her skills and interests were taught to her by her grandfather, a prospector who hunted for gold, uranium, precious metals, and minerals. She is passing this legacy on to her nephew, Perry Butler, who, at the age of eleven, is already an accomplished rockhound and gold prospector, as well as a published author.

Gail is a contributing editor to *Rock & Gem* magazine and has written many articles on rockhounding, gold prospecting, lapidary, and other subjects for this and other publications. One of her most unique writing experiences occurred when she was asked to write an article on dowsing for a Greek publication, *News on Minerals*. When the article was published, a copy was sent to her. She was unable to read a word of it. It was truly Greek to her.

Gail has recently retired from the Los Angeles County Sheriff's Department where she worked as a deputy sheriff for twenty years.

Gail plans and departs for her adventures, explorations, and expeditions from her home in Upland, California.

INDEX